Ask the Horse!

— And More Stories My Guru Told Me

Ask the Horse!

— And More Stories My Guru Told Me

Retold by

Swami Prakashananda

Sarasvati Productions

Ask the Horse!
— And More Stories My Guru Told Me

© 2008 by Swami Prakashananda

Published by:
Sarasvati Productions
1625 Hollingsworth Dr.
Mountain View, CA 94040 (USA)

www.SarasvatiProductions.com

Printed in the United States of America
First Printing 2008

Cover Design by Gargi of Di Maria Design

ISBN 978-1-886140-14-1
Library of Congress Control Number: 2008907121

Other books by Swami Prakashananda

Baba Muktananda – A Biography
Don't Think of a Monkey

Table of Contents

Preface

It has been fourteen years (1994) since the first collection of 108 stories was published under the title, *Don't Think of a Monkey and Other Stories My Guru Told Me*. Unfortunately that book is now out of print. Over the years I have heard from many readers telling me how much they enjoyed the stories and asked for more. This second collection of 108 stories is the outcome of their request.

Like my Guru, Baba Muktananda, I too have always enjoyed a good story. My encounter with Hindu story telling began in 1969 while traveling in Northern India. There I met a Brahmin family who invited me to stay in their home for sometime. The father began to teach me about Hinduism with the aid of various stories. His wife too would instruct me using stories while she prepared meals for her family. Story telling has long been an integral part in the transmission of Hindu thought. We find that many Hindu tales have migrated into Islamic and European cultures over the centuries. For example, the tales from the Arabian Nights were mainly influenced by the tradition of the *Panchatantra* and the Buddhist *Jataka* Tales. In fact, the tales from the Panchatantra—meaning "Five Books"—have traveled the world in numerous translations for over two millenniums.

I read India's two great epics, the *Ramayana* and *Mahabharata*, as well as many of the 18 Maha-Puranas which are filled with countless stories about human beings, sages, gods and demons. Once while waiting in Katmandu, Nepal, for a visa to return to India, I spent many hours in the local library reading books on Hindu literature which included a ten volume set called, *Katha Sarit Sagara* or "*The Ocean of*

Story." It was written in the 11th century by the Kashmirian poet, Somadeva. I have read the *Panchatantra* and many of the *Jataka* tales or Buddhist birth stories which describe the Buddha's previous lives. I have read many stories narrated by modern teachers, authors, and speakers. One of my favorites, as well as my Guru's, was Swami Rama Tirtha. Another is Shri Ramakrishna Paramahamsa. Of course my own Guru was a master story teller as well.

Besides Hindu teaching stories, I have also read stories from the Jewish, Christian, Sufi, Buddhist and Taoist traditions. Obviously my Guru had also read stories from various traditions as is reflected in this and the previous collection of stories. I must, however, mention here that although the majority of stories in this collection were used by my Guru in his talks not all are. I have added a few other stories that I have come across over the years and have found meaningful. Like the first collection, there are quite a few stories of the inscrutable Mullah Nasrudin, whom my Baba often referred to as, "My Friend ..."

In closing, I would like to offer my respect and gratitude to all the authors and transmitters of such stories, both ancient and modern. They have certainly enriched my life through their insights into human nature and life's conditions which are often presented in a humorous way.

I also wish to specially thank Gargi Di Maria for her beautiful cover illustration and design, and my editor, Diane (Sita) Dropik.

A note to the reader. All non-English words are italicized the first time used. Although their meanings are usually given in the story, a glossary follows the text.

The Frogs in the Well

O nce there was a frog who traveled to many distant lands. His original home was the ocean, but as he was adventurous, he decided to wander around the world visiting different water spots.

On one of his travels, he stopped near a village of frogs who were out sunning themselves on large flat rocks. This community of frogs all lived in a nearby well. It was a huge well and very deep. The village frogs welcomed the stranger and inquired about his travels. They were filled with amazement as the traveler related how other frogs lived around the world. They asked him about his own home, and he told them about the ocean and tried to describe to them its scenery and size. But the local frogs could not quite understand this idea about the ocean.

"Is your ocean larger than that pool of water?" the village frog asked while pointing to a nearby large pot hole.

The traveler smiled and said, "Oh yes brother, it is much larger than that."

As it was the rainy season, there were many puddles of water, large and small, and pointing to a much larger collection of water the village frog asked, "Is the ocean larger than that pond?"

The ocean frog answered, "Yes my friends, the ocean is much bigger than any of these puddles, much larger."

The village frogs were still not able to grasp the vastness of the ocean. They said, "Come with us, we'll show you our home."

Arriving at the edge of the well, the chief frog said, "This is our home, we all live here together. But even with our large population there is plenty of room, and we can also travel to great depths. How much smaller is the ocean in relation to this large body of water?" he asked.

The traveler again smiled and said, "My brother, the ocean is much larger than this well, in fact, many thousands of wells this size can be swallowed up by the ocean. The ocean is so vast how can I describe it? All the land that you see around you, as far as you can see, imagine that to be all water—the ocean is still larger," explained the stranger.

The leader of the frogs became very angry upon hearing this statement from the stranger, and said, "We have welcomed you into our village, and now you repay us with lies? How is it possible for all that water to exist? You try to insult us by such ridiculous stories about an ocean! Leave us quickly or we will feed you to the snakes," shouted the chief frog, while the other frogs croaked loudly, expressing their displeasure.

The poor traveler tried to explain further, but he was threatened with bodily harm and was chased out of the village. This is the human condition as well. Everyone sees only their own little pond, and believe it to be the extent of the universe.

The Brahmin and the Evil Spirit

Once a *brahmin* approached a sage who was reputed to have the power of controlling spirits. He thought that if he could control a spirit, he would be able to fulfill his desires for wealth and happiness. The sage advised him to give up such intentions, explaining that although it may be possible to obtain material prosperity through the help of a spirit, there was also the possibility of great harm. Nevertheless, the brahmin was determined and did not heed the sage's advice. So seeing the *brahmin's* determination, the sage finally agreed to instruct him. He initiated the brahmin, with the spirit controlling mantra, and then instructed him on the proper method of meditation.

The brahmin started practicing according to the Guru's instructions, and within a short period, a fierce looking spirit suddenly appeared before him.

"Why have you called me?" thundered the spirit.

"You are to stay with me as my servant and carry out all my orders without disagreement," replied the brahmin.

"All right," replied the spirit, "I will agree to your proposal, however, you too will have to enter into a contract with me. I am not to remain idle for a single moment without some work. If you fail to give me a task, I will destroy all the things previously done by me, and I will destroy you as well. Do you agree with this contract?" snarled the spirit.

"I have enough desires to last a lifetime," the brahmin said, "so yes, I agree to your terms. My first instructions to you is that since I have no home build me a fine house, with lovely gardens and a water pond containing exotic fishes."

At his command, the spirit immediately constructed a beautiful mansion finishing in a single day what would have normally taken many months of work. The brahmin thought, "I now have a beautiful mansion but no wealth," so he commanded the spirit to bring him great wealth. Within a moment, the spirit brought the brahmin immense wealth consisting of valuable gems, gold, and silver.

In this way, the spirit fulfilled all the material desires of the brahmin within only a few days. The spirit insisted on more work, but the brahmin was unable to give him any.

"According to our agreement," the spirit reminded the brahmin, "I will now have to destroy all your belongings and kill you too."

The brahmin seeing the spirit approaching him with eyes full of rage ran for his life. Out of breath, he soon arrived at his Guru's ashram, and falling at his feet spoke with folded hands, "Save me my Lord, or I shall be killed by this evil spirit."

Hearing the pathetic cry of his disciple, the Guru said, "My child, do not be afraid. I warned you that there is great danger in trying to control spirits. However, go home and drive a bamboo pole in the middle of your courtyard and command the spirit to move constantly up and down the pole. Then that mischievous spirit will not be able to harm you."

Upon hearing his Guru's advice, the brahmin immediately returned home and did what he was instructed. The spirit, from then on, was made to continuously climb up and down the bamboo pole. Exhausted from doing the same work without relief, the spirit finally said to the brahmin, "My lord, give me permission to leave. Whatever I have accomplished for you shall be yours and I will cause you no harm." The brahmin hearing the words of the spirit, happily released him, and henceforth lived in peace.

The mind is like that spirit. If it is not given something to preoccupy itself, it causes all kinds of havoc. It can never remain still for a single moment. Through imagination, it creates and pollutes many things. Instability is its very nature. As the seeker tries to immerse himself in meditation, letting go of all outer activities, the spirit-like mind having no work to do then turns on the person by projecting various desires and impulses. The spirit-like mind must be made to travel up and down the sushumna nadi (the bamboo pole in the body), between the Muladhara and Sahasrara centers. Eventually, it will be compelled to leave of its own accord, and one becomes immune to all desires.

Fighting Over Grapes

Once a Persian, a Turk, a Greek and an Arab were traveling through the Middle East together. Although, they did not know each other's language very well, they had managed to communicate to a certain extent by different gestures.

After traveling for sometime, they became hungry, but unfortunately they had only one *dinar* between themselves.

The Turk suggested, "Let us purchase some *ujalas*."

"No," said the Persian, "we should purchase some *ungur* instead."

The Arab became excited and said, "We will buy *inab* with this money."

But the Greek said, "You are all silly, we should buy only *staafylia* with the little money we have."

Each of them kept voicing their own preferences and soon the conversation became heated. At one point, it became so intense that blows were about to be struck. But just then a wise man happened to pass by and seeing the commotion he asked what they were arguing about.

They explained to him their disagreement and the wise man, being familiar with all four languages said, "If you are willing to give me the *dinar*, I believe I can solve your problem."

The four men agreed and the wise man went to the market and purchased a *dinar's* worth of grapes and returned with them. When the four travelers saw the grapes, they all shouted with delight.

"Oh, my *inab!*" said the Arab.

"*Ungur!*" shouted the Persian.

"My *Ujala!*" cried the Turk.

"Oh *Staafylia!*" the Greek said.

"Thank you!" they all chimed in unison, for indeed they all wanted grapes all along.

The great Sufi Julal-ud-Din Rumi used to tell this story to his disciples in order to convey to them that in fact everyone desires the same thing, God's joy. But because of various languages and customs, people speak of it in their own way. Since we do not always know each other's ways, we argue and fight amongst ourselves.

You Can't Please Everyone!

Once Mullah Nasrudin and his son went on a journey. Nasrudin wanted to walk and so he placed his son on the donkey while he walked ahead.

Along the way, they passed some travelers and as they passed by them they overheard one of the travelers say, "Look at that healthy young boy on the donkey. That is today's youth. They show no respect for their elders. He rides while his poor father walks."

Hearing these words, the boy felt ashamed and got off the donkey and insisted that his father ride while he walked. So Nasrudin got on the donkey and the boy walked by his side.

Soon they met another group. "Will you look at that?" one of them said. "That poor boy has to walk while his father rides the donkey."

Hearing this, Nasrudin picked up the boy and seated him on the donkey in front, while he sat behind. And they continued on their way.

Soon they met another group of people. "Look at that poor donkey! He has to carry the weight of two people."

Hearing this, the Mullah said to his son, "I think the best

solution is if we both walk. Then no one can complain."

So they continued on their journey on foot, with the donkey walking behind them.

Again they met another group of people. "Look at these two fools!" one of them said. "They have a donkey and yet they are both walking in the hot sun. You would think that they would be smart enough to ride their donkey."

Hearing this, Nasrudin turned to his son and said, "This just goes to show that you can't escape people's criticism, and therefore you can't please everyone." And so they gave up the hope of trying to please everyone.

I heard another version of this story, but instead of Mullah Nasrudin and his son on a journey, it is Lord Rama and his wife Sita who are on a journey. Here's how it goes:

Once Lord Rama, the king of Ayodhya, was on a journey with his wife Sita. There was only one horse, Rama was riding it, while Sita walked behind him.

As they approached a small village, Rama overheard criticism of his riding the horse while his poor wife walked behind him. And feeling the stings of the villagers criticism, he dismounted and placed his wife on the horse. They then continued on their journey.

After sometime they reached another village. But as the villagers saw them, they too became critical saying amongst themselves: "No king should be made to walk while a horse is available.

This is a disgrace."

As they continued further, Rama reflected on the criticism he had just heard and decided to ride the horse along with Sita. But shortly, they arrived at another village. When the villagers saw the royal couple, both riding the horse, they began to talk amongst themselves saying, "Look at how they abuse that creature! Have they no compassion for that poor horse?"

And so, the moral is the same, you can't please everyone!

The King and the Maiden

Once there was a great king. He was known throughout his kingdom as a just and righteous ruler. It so happened that once, during his birthday celebration, he ordered all his servants and others in his palace to ask for whatever they wished for. Now some asked for gold, precious gems, and property, while others asked for promotions. True to his word, the king granted all their desires.

But as the king was walking across the courtyard, he noticed a maid-servant standing quietly in a remote corner of the palace. She was dressed in rags and appeared sad and withdrawn. The king walked over to her and asked what was the matter. "Don't you know it's my birthday today?" he asked. "Everyone is celebrating, so why are you so sad?" the king inquired kindly.

The girl did not say anything, so the king continued questioning her trying to change her mood. He said, "Everyone has made a request, which I have fulfilled. What do you wish for the most?" the king inquired. "Tell me and I will fulfill it."

The girl now answered and said, "I do indeed have a wish my lord, but I wonder if you are in a position to grant it?"

"Anything," the king answered. "Just ask and I will grant it."

The maid then smiled and said, "If that is so, your majesty, then extend your hand to confirm your promise."

As he did so, the girl grabbed the king's hand and said, "Your Majesty, I wish for nothing else but you in marriage. Will you be able to grant this willingly?" the girl asked.

The king was obviously taken by surprise at this request, but, he had given her his word, and so, he married the poor maid-servant, who soon became a queen.

In the same way, God fulfills all our desires. But, everyone only wishes for a few coins or some polished stones, a piece of earth, or some other trivial object. Instead, if like the wise maid-servant we desire nothing but God Himself, then everything else will be at our disposal.

The Intoxicated Bee

There was once a bee who was intoxicated with his youth. He flew from flower to flower drinking the juice of each flower. He was intoxicated with the flowers' nectar and did not know how the days and nights passed. One day, he came across a lake full of lotus flowers. He settled in one of the flowers and started drinking its sweet nectar. He thought he should return to the hive and inform the other bees of his delicious find, but he became so intoxicated that he kept thinking that he had plenty of time. "Just a little more nectar before I go," he thought to himself.

He was so engrossed in drinking the juice that he did not notice that the sun had set and the flower's petals began to close. Before he knew it, the petals had closed completely. "What does it matter," the bee thought, "the night will pass quickly, and in the morning when the sun rises, the petals will open again and I'll fly out. Meanwhile, I'll continue to enjoy myself. Tomorrow I'll go and tell everyone about my great discovery, and they can also join me." Thinking in this way, the bee continued drinking the sweet juice throughout the night.

But as destiny would have it, during the night a herd of elephants came to the lake to drink water. Seeing the many lotus flowers, they began plucking them and throwing them into their mouths. Soon the lotus, in which the bee was in, was also plucked and eaten bringing an end to his life; as well as to all his plans to return to his friends and family.

This story of the bee is found in the writings of Bhartrihari. He was a saint who was formally a king, who renounced his throne, turning the kingdom over to his son. He wanted to practice meditation in a solitary cave in the forest. Just like the bee, we too are foolishly attached to our desires never realizing the impending danger just ahead. Instead of spending our time in this world discovering ourselves, we remain constantly engrossed in sense pleasures. Soon the elephant of death arrives, and we wonder what we have accomplished. The bee could have escaped, even after being trapped inside the lotus. He could have easily burrowed through its petals, but he was too intoxicated with the flower's nectar. Bhartrihari instructs us to meditate on the inner Self, while we are still young and before old age and disease sets in. Some think that they will perform spiritual practices when they are old, but Bhartrihari says that we should not behave like a man who frantically rushes about trying to dig a well when his house is already on fire.

Everyone Is Right

Once while the local magistrate was on vacation, Nasrudin was asked to serve as the magistrate.

Now it so happened that one of his neighbors came with a complaint against a fellow neighbor.

Nasrudin listened to the neighbor's complaint very carefully and stroking his beard, he said, "Yes, you are quite right."

Then he heard the defendant's version, and again he listened very carefully and said, "Yes, you are quite right."

The Mullah's wife overhearing the entire proceedings, said to him, "O Nasrudin, how can this be? They can't both be right."

"Yes, dear wife," replied Nasrudin, "you are quite right."

The Sadhu and His Blanket

Once a *sadhu* was traveling on a pilgrimage when he stopped in a local temple for the night. Now this sadhu had only a blanket as his possession, and he spread it over himself and went to sleep. That night a thief came and stole a number of items from the temple and also took the poor sadhu's blanket.

The next day the temple authorities reported the theft to the police and a search was made for the thief. After a few days, the thief was caught and brought before the judge. The judge was given a list of objects stolen from the temple, and he asked those in the courtroom, "Are there any other complaints against this thief?"

The sadhu, who was also sitting in the courtroom, got up and told the judge, "Yes your honor, there are other charges. This man has stolen my hat, he has taken my shawl, as well as my pants, and he has also stolen my blanket."

Burning with resentment and fearing that the sadhu would be awarded all the objects mentioned, the thief jumped to his feet and said, "Your honor, I confess to having taken this man's blanket, but I have not stolen the other objects he mentions."

The judge turned to the sadhu and said, "What do you have to say about this?"

The sadhu replied, "Your honor, it is true that he has stolen my blanket, but to me it was everything. When I wrapped it around my head in the intense noon sun, it became a hat; when I wore it over my shoulders, it was a shawl. If I wrapped it around my waist, it became my pants, and when I laid it over me at night, it became my blanket. Therefore, he has indeed stolen all these objects I mentioned."

The Precious Gem
And the Piece of Glass

Once a brahmin went to the forest to practice penance in order to obtain the precious wish-fulfilling gem called *Chintamani*. Through God's grace, within only a few days the invaluable gem appeared before him. But on seeing it, he thought, "Is this really the wish-fulfilling gem? What penance have I done that I should obtain it so soon? I must not touch it, for it may be transformed into a piece of glass."

After thinking in this way, the brahmin concluded, "This can not be the real green *Chintamani*, otherwise it would have appeared only after a long period of arduous penance." The moment he said this, the wish-fulfilling gem disappeared.

Time passed and one day, while absorbed in meditation, some boys passed the brahmin and playfully threw a green piece of glass near him. After finishing his meditation and opening his eyes, he saw the glass and became delighted. He thought, "Through the grace of God, the object of my devotion is fulfilled after many days of austerities." Thinking that all his sorrows had ended by obtaining the wish-fulfilling gem, the brahmin returned to his home and sold all his possessions and traveled to a distant land. But fortune was not to be his. The brahmin learned that the stone was only glass. And so his sorrows truly began.

This story from the Yoga Vasishtha explains what happens when rare things are easily gained. Instead of testing the true wish-fulfilling gem, it is discarded as worthless, and a worthless piece of glass is accepted as valuable. Our experiences should be tested by the touchstone of the heart, and if they concur with the Guru's instructions, as well as scriptural injunctions, then there can be no room for doubt. Doubt brings distress and misery to the seeker and draws him away from the spiritual path. Due to the lack of faith in one's Guru, or the scriptures, the Bhagavad Gita says that the doubtful person can never obtain happiness in this world or in the next.

There Is No One Like My Rama

Long ago, in a previous age, the great hero Rama defeated the demon Ravana on his island kingdom of Sri Lanka after he had kidnapped his wife Sita. While he was returning from Sri Lanka with Sita and Hanuman in the aerial ship called *Pushpak,* Hanuman who was deeply devoted to Rama, began to think to himself, "There is no one like my Rama."

Reading Hanuman's mind, Rama decided to teach him a lesson. Just at that very moment, Sita was handing over Rama's ring, when it accidentally dropped into the sea below. Rama shouted, "Quick, Hanuman, go find the ring." Without hesitation, the great monkey dove into the deep ocean. But when he reached the bottom, he was surprised to find a large pile of rings exactly like the one Sita had just dropped. And to make matters worse, they were all inscribed with the name 'Rama' on them. Hanuman was perplexed and could not tell which of the rings belonged to *his* Rama.

Seeing an old fish swimming nearby, Hanuman asked him about the pile of rings, hoping that he could guide him. "Take any ring you like," replied the old fish, "there have been many Ramas like your Rama. At the end of every third age, a Rama is born. Each one passes this way on his return home from defeating the evil king Ravana, and each time a ring is dropped, thereby creating this large pile. So, pick any one you like, they are all the same."

It often happens that some disciples become trapped in the idea that their Guru is the only real Guru. Of course, one should surrender themselves completely to one Guru, but this does not mean that they should be disrespectful towards others. All great saints and sages are manifestations of the same Truth. They do not say anything new but all proclaim the same eternal Truth.

Don't Become Anything!

Once a Guru and his disciple were on a pilgrimage together. Throughout the journey, the old Guru would keep telling his disciple, "Never become anything. If you remember this rule and don't become anything, you will never experience any difficulties in life."

They continued on their pilgrimage and one day, while traveling through a forest, they came across a beautiful empty cottage. But this was actually a hunting lodge belonging to the local king. When they went inside, they found a beautifully decorated bedroom with two large beds. The disciple asked, "Gurudev, will it be all right if we sleep here tonight?"

"It will be all right," replied the Guru. But he warned his disciple by saying, "make sure that you don't become anything while you are sleeping."

"Why would I become anything while I'm asleep?" wondered the disciple. But feeling tired, he laid down on one of the beds, while the Guru laid on the other. They were soon fast asleep.

Now it so happened that the king was out hunting that day, and soon returned to the cottage with his guards. When he walked into the bedroom, he was astonished to see the two ragged men sleeping soundly on the royal beds. The king went over to the bed where the Guru was lying and shook him. The old man opened his eyes and looked at the king, but he soon closed them again pretending to be asleep. The king shook him again and shouted, "Who are you? Where did you come from?"

The old man remained silent. The king thought that he was an imbecile and ordered his guards to carry him outside and put him down somewhere.

The king next went over to the other bed and shook the disciple while shouting, "Who are you? Why are you here? How dare you sleep on the royal bed?"

The disciple was startled, and forgetting the Guru's instructions, he angrily replied, "How dare you speak to me that way? I am a *swami* and the disciple of a great Guru."

The king became infuriated and yelled, "You are a scoundrel and your Guru must be one as well." He ordered his guards to take him outside and give him a good thrashing.

As the disciple laid groaning on the path outside the cottage, he noticed his Guru sleeping peacefully under a nearby tree. He managed to crawl over to the Guru, and after waking him up he began to complain saying, "O Gurudev, they beat me mercilessly and kicked me many times. My whole body is black and blue from the beating. How could this have happened?" he asked disheartened.

"Why did they beat you?" the Guru asked in surprise, "They did not beat me. You must have become something. What did you say to them?"

"I told them that I was a *swami* and the disciple of a great Guru," answered the disciple.

"Aah!" sighed the old Guru, "Just as I thought. Didn't I warn you that if you became anything you would get into trouble. If you would have only followed my instructions, nothing would have happened to you. Since I did not claim to be anything, nothing happened to me."

Such is the nature of the ego. It is always attempting to make us become something other than what we are. Along with ego comes arrogance, which in turn brings grief. If we are like the immature disciple and add something more to the pure "I" consciousness, we become troubled by life's circumstances. If, like the wise Master, we remain simply as the pure Self, without any further additions, then nothing will bother us in this world. The ego of discipleship overpowered the disciple's intelligence, and he started acting arrogant and boastful. This does not mean that one should not assert themselves in life. It means that one should be aware of their own actions and be prepared to endure their consequences. If one acts with arrogance, the results may be drastic. Unlike the disciple, the Guru had eradicated his ego and any arrogance and so did not become anything. But the disciple forgot the Master's teaching, and the moment he was questioned, his ego immediately forced him to become something. He thought that he had special rights; however, the king did not think so. Therefore, don't become anything but always remain your own pure inner Self.

The Necklace Which Was Never Lost

There was once a girl who owned a beautiful necklace. She always wore the necklace around her neck. One day as she was taking her bath, she heard a procession passing by in front of her home. She got out of the bath tub and dressed quickly and ran to her balcony to see the procession.

After the procession passed, she went back inside and sat in front of a mirror to comb her hair. As she was combing her hair, she suddenly noticed that her necklace was missing. She began shouting, "My necklace is missing. I lost my necklace."

Upon hearing the girl's shouts, her neighbors ran to her apartment asking what had happened.

"I lost my beautiful necklace," sobbed the girl.

"Where did you last see it?" asked one of the neighbors.

"Oh I don't know," she said a bit confused, "I could have placed it anywhere."

One of her friends placed her hands around the girl's neck and started feeling around. She soon felt some object underneath the blouse and said, "What is this?"

The girl placed her hands on the object and opened her blouse, suddenly she shrieked, "I found my necklace."

This is an old story told in Vedantic literature to illustrate how, even though divinity lies right within ourselves, and in fact is our own inner essence, we think that it has become lost and is located somewhere else. Even though the girl thought her necklace was lost, in fact it was never actually lost at all. In the same way, Vedanta says that the Self is never lost nor is it something to be regained. It is in fact who we are all along.

The Lord's Boon

There were once two men who were close friends. One was blind and the other lame. Being friends, they helped each other: the blind man carried the lame man on his shoulders, while the lame man directed the blind man's way.

So the friendship was good for both of them. But as time went by they had a falling out. And as it often happens when friends have a falling out, they became the bitterest of enemies.

One day God sent for the lame man and since he had performed some good deeds in a previous life, asked him to choose a boon. But instead of asking for his legs to be restored, the lame man said, "Oh God, please deprive that blind fellow of his legs."

God then sent for the blind man and like-wise asked him to ask for a boon. The blind man replied, "Please God, take the light out of the eyes of that lame man."

Unfortunately, this reflects the character and conditions of many in our modern society. God's boon is difficult to achieve, yet instead of benefiting from it, we wish to use it to do harm to others.

First a Thief, Then a Sage
Valmiki - India's First Poet

A long time ago, towards the end of the third age according to Hindu astronomical calendars, there lived a thief and murderer named Ratnakar (others give the name Vali and Prachetasa). He had robbed and harassed hundreds of people and is even said to have killed dozens of them. He would hide in a dark forest located near the foothills of the Himalayas waiting to rob unsuspecting travelers. It is said that Ratnakar was born into a good family, but he had fallen in with the wrong crowd and human life meant nothing to him. He did not give even a second thought when taking it.

One day, while lying in wait, he saw two sages enter the forest. He followed them silently for some time preparing to pounce on them. The sages soon came to a clearing in the forest, and there they sat quietly under a large and ancient Banyan tree. Ratnakar came closer to where the sages were sitting and swiftly attacked them and caught hold of both sages.

One of the sages was Narada, and he said, "Ratnakar, you can have whatever we possess, but first please answer one question: Why do you pursue in this line of work?"

At first the thief was taken aback, as he did not know how they knew his name. But he answered saying, "I follow this line of work for the sake of my family. They would otherwise starve."

"I see," said Narada with an air of surprise, "Then they will of course share in the fruit of your many sins?" inquired the sage.

"Of course they will," the thief replied. "As they have shared in my fortunes, they will of course be happy to share in my burdens as well."

"So you really believe this?" Narada asked somewhat doubtful. "Well, go and ask them," said Narada, "we shall remain at this spot until you return. Then you can do whatever you like to us."

Ratnakar thought for a moment, his mind confused by the challenge. Finally he agreed and returned to his home. On his way, the thief's mind was pondering on what his family's response would be. When he reached his home, he called his family together and asked, "Will you bear with me the fruits of my sins?"

"How can I share in your sins?" asked the wife. "It is your duty to support us. Besides, it is you who has chosen this profession."

The children also offered no support, claiming they were too young to be of any help.

Hearing his family's response and remembering the many sins he had committed, Ratnakar became filled with panic and dread. He immediately rushed back to the forest, and reaching there he threw himself at the sage's feet crying, "No one will share in my sins. Please help me and tell me what I should do."

Narada gazed at the thief for a few moments, as if looking into his future. He then said, "Repeat God's sacred name of '*Rama*'. As it is full of life and joy, repeating this name with deep concentration, in time it will destroy all your sins."

Ratnakar attempted to repeat the holy name, but his sins were so intense, he could not pronounce the two syllables correctly. Narada saw his difficulty and said, "Instead, you should repeat the word '*Mara, Mara*.'" Since the murderer was familiar with this word, as it meant death, he had no trouble repeating it.

The thief sat down and started repeating "Mara, Mara, Mara" in a low murmur. Soon he became absorbed in the mantra, and he sat still for many days—then months passed. As he continued repeating the mantra with deep concentration, the syllables 'Ma-ra' soon became transformed into 'Ra-ma'.

As this occurred, he entered a deeper level of consciousness and became full of joy. He remained deeply absorbed for many years without even a twitch in his body. Soon, white ants began building their home around his still body.

As he became invisible, all that one could hear was the occasional sigh of "Rama, Rama, Rama" coming from the anthill. After about twelve years, the two sages once again passed through that forest. They searched for the old thief, but they could not locate him. Then suddenly they heard the sweet sound of "Rama, Rama, Rama" coming from the nearby anthill. They went over to it and tore down the anthill to free the old thief. Narada whispered something into his ear, and soon he came out of his deep meditation. He was now no longer the old thief but had been transformed into a great sage. Narada was pleased with his disciple and gave him a new name. As he had come out of the white anthill he called him *Valmiki*.

From his deep meditation and the blessings of his Guru, Valmiki also gained poetic inspiration. To this day, he is remembered as India's first master poet. He settled on the banks of the river Tamasa where he was later inspired to write India's first epic, the Ramayana, which is the life and acts of Lord Rama. He wrote the epic in a beautiful and new poetic style. Today the story of the Ramayana is known throughout the world in one form or another.

A True Disciple

There was once a seeker who used to ask Kabir, "Please describe what a true disciple should be like." But each time Kabir remained silent, so the seeker continued to ask the same question whenever he had the opportunity.

On one occasion, during a celebration where many people had gathered around Kabir, that same seeker again asked the question. Now Kabir did not answer him directly, but he looked around and then called one of his disciples named Kamal. Kabir instructed Kamal to bring some *mava* which is made from solidified milk. Normally sugar is added and then distributed as *prasad* to the guests. But instead of asking Kamal to add sugar, Kabir told him to flavor it with salt.

Without hesitation Kamal added the salt and brought it to Kabir. Kabir handed it to the seeker who had asked the question, and asked him to distribute it to everyone there. Kabir then returned to his weaving without saying another word.

Kabir continued working at his loom. After sometime, he happened to drop the shuttle. Kabir again called Kamal and said, "I have dropped my shuttle, please bring the large lamp so we can find it."

Although it was broad daylight, Kamal lit the lamp and brought it to his Guru. "Please try to find it," Kabir told Kamal.

Holding the lamp up high, as one would normally do at night, Kamal searched for the shuttle. After finding it, he handed it to his master and once again retired to some other duty. As there were many people watching, they all began to wonder what was going on. Some even thought that both Kabir and Kamal had lost their minds. They reasoned that in Kabir's case it was understandable since he was an old man and probably could not see very well, but Kamal was a young and intelligent man. So why did Kabir tell him to add salt to the *mava*, and why did Kamal follow his instructions without question? Everyone thought it was very strange, but no one said anything. Meanwhile, Kabir had returned to his weaving, as if nothing had happened.

The seeker, who had not heard an answer to his question, again asked Kabir, "Please describe what a true disciple should be like."

"Do you not understand yet what a true disciple should be like?" asked Kabir. "A disciple should be like Kamal," he continued. "Just because Kamal follows my instructions implicitly, don't assume that he does not know that sugar should be added to *mava* and not salt. He added salt only because I had asked him to do so. And he certainly knows that a lamp is not needed to find an object in broad daylight. He brought a lamp because I asked him to. Kamal is a true disciple. He obeys the command of the Guru with the utmost obedience. This is how a true disciple should be like."

Now We Are Even!

One day Mullah Nasrudin went to a Turkish bath-house. As he was poorly dressed, the attendants gave him an old bathrobe and a raggedy towel and ignored him the whole time he was there.

When Nasrudin left, he gave each of the attendants a gold coin as a tip. Since he had not complained about the poor service, they were surprised, and wondered how much more he would have given them if they had treated him better.

The next week Nasrudin again visited the bath house. This time however the attendants could not do enough for him. They brought him an embroidered robe, fresh towels, massaged and perfumed his whole body.

After his massage was over and he was leaving, he gave each of the attendants the smallest copper coin as a tip.

"What is this?" the attendants asked in surprise, "Last week you gave us each a gold coin, but today, after all we have done, you give us such a small tip?"

"Don't be upset," said the Mullah. "Today's tip is for last week's service, while last week's gold coin was for today's service. Now we are even."

Mohini and the Demon

There was once a demon who began performing intense austerities. His aim was to obtain a boon of power from Lord Shiva. After a long period passed, Shiva appeared to the demon and asked what he desired.

"May all that I touch be instantly turned into ashes," said the demon.

"So be it," replied Shiva with a smile.

It was no doubt a foolish boon but no matter, for Shiva is the embodiment of generosity. However, the moment the boon was granted, the demon rushed towards Shiva himself hoping to place his hand on his head making him his first victim. But Shiva was too clever and suddenly shrank himself to the size of a tiny insect and hid inside a mango.

Now the gods were powerless to stop the demon since he could easily turn them into ashes with the mere touch of his finger. They therefore approached Vishnu, the Sustainer of the universe, and prayed that he relieve them of their enemy.

Vishnu agreed to their request with a nod and a smile on his lips. Contemplating for a moment his strategy, Vishnu transformed himself into a beautiful maiden named Mohini and approached the demon. The moment the demon saw her, he immediately fell madly in love with her. The beautiful Mohini began to dance around the demon but avoided getting too close. She soon had him imitating her every gesture. As she twirled about, the demon twirled about. When she kicked up her heels, the demon kicked up his heels. She touched her head, the demon touched his head—and immediately was turned into ashes.

Counting Crows

O
ccasionally Akbar used to enjoy posing questions to his courtiers which were thought to be unanswerable. But to Akbar's constant delight, Birbal always had an answer, no matter how strange the question. So one day, the king took his seat on his throne as usual, then asked in a grave tone, "Tell me quickly: how many crows are there in all of Agra? This is very important," he added, "so it better be accurate, otherwise there will be trouble."

The courtiers stared at each other in fear. Some said that they knew the approximate number of elephants, while others knew how many horses there were, but no one seemed to know the number of crows. They all became anxious and wondered what to do. Only Birbal remained calm. Then, after a few moments, with a smile on his lips he said, "Your Majesty, there are exactly sixteen thousand, three hundred and forty-two crows in all of Agra."

"Are you certain?" asked Akbar suspiciously. "Don't try to bluff your way out of this one, Birbal. We will have an accurate investigation to confirm your count."

"Yes of course," Birbal said confidently. "However," he added, "I can't guarantee that all the crows will remain in the city before the count can be taken. Some may decide to visit their families or friends in other cities, in which case there will of course be fewer crows than the number I have given. Or, perhaps friends and relatives will visit those crows who live here in the city. In that case there will be more crows in the city than the number I have given. I can only guarantee that at this very moment there are sixteen thousand, three hundred and forty-two crows in Agra."

The king suddenly burst out laughing, and all the courtiers joined him. "Aah Birbal," the king sighed, "you are indeed amazing."

Ask The Horse!

Throughout his life Nasrudin used to always ride a donkey. Wherever he went this was his mode of transportation. But Nasrudin had a secret desire. He wanted to ride a horse. He had been thinking about it for a long time. So one day he decided to purchase one. However, not knowing anything about horses, the owner of the horse sold him a spirited animal.

Now of course Nasrudin had never been on a horse in his life and so he did not know how to ride the animal. But being proud of his new horse, he decided to ride him through town, so all of his friends could see him. But as he came near a vegetable seller, the horse tried to eat some of his carrots, so the vendor picked up a stick and gave the horse two blows. Suddenly the horse bolted and Nasrudin was practically thrown off, but as he was falling, he managed to wrap his arms around the horse's neck. The horse was running out of control and Nasrudin looked quite comical riding upside down with his legs and arms wrapped around the horse's neck, he was holding on for dear life.

Seeing him in this condition, a friend yelled out, "Oh Nasrudin, where are you going in such a hurry?"

"I don't know," Nasrudin shouted back, "ask the horse!"

In the same way, we too may ask ourselves, "where are we going?" The answer would have to be, "I don't know, ask my mind!" My Guru would say: "If I ask where are you going, you would say, 'don't ask me, ask society.' And if we ask society where it is going, society would say, 'We don't know. We are going where everyone else is going.'" Baba would often tell this story to illustrate how people blindly follow the whims of their minds, and by extension, those of society. He would say that one should not follow anything blindly and would ask: where was our modern culture, with all its technology, really leading us? He would often replace Nasrudin's answer with, "I don't know, ask the culture!"

Kabir and the Buffalo

Once, a seeker named Ram Das approached the great saint Kabir. With tears in his eyes, he bowed at the saints' feet and said, "Oh Kabir, you have the ability to perform miracles so kindly bless me that I may see God."

Kabir was moved by the sincerity of the seeker, and after reflecting for a moment, he told the young man that he would show him God in three days. After giving him some further instructions on how to prepare himself, Kabir told the seeker he could go.

The next day, the young man sold all his property and purchased the necessary goods needed to prepare a grand feast for the occasion. All types of delicious foods were prepared and many prominent guests were invited to attend the ceremonies. Finally on the third day, while everyone was participating in the ceremonies, Ram Das sat absorbed in meditation with the hope of soon having a vision of God.

The guests were told that food would be served only after God had appeared before Ram Das. Therefore, they all waited with baited breath. But soon noon came and went, and yet there was no sign of God. After a number of more hours passed, God still did not appear. Some of the guests began to complain that they were hungry. A few even blamed Kabir and thought that Ram Das was a fool for believing that he would see God. But some still believed that God would appear and thought themselves blessed to be witnesses to such an event. Nevertheless, everyone was anxiously waiting for God to appear.

In the meantime, there was a commotion in the kitchen. Somehow a buffalo had gotten inside and was causing havoc. He was knocking over the pots and even started tasting some of the sweet dishes. With his bulky frame, he damaged the oven, and soon the food was being trampled under his hoofs mixing it with his dung. The cooks were all shouting at the beast, and there was chaos everywhere.

Since the buffalo was causing havoc, the guests became infuriated, and even Ram Das became angry. Everyone surrounded the buffalo hoping to drive him out before he did further damages. At that point, Ram Das picked up a staff and started beating the poor animal mercilessly wounding him badly. The guests also started cursing Kabir blaming him for the whole mess and for fooling them in this way.

The wounded buffalo, crying and bleeding from deep gashes inflicted by Ram Das, managed to escape and ran outside to the garden where Kabir happened to be seated. Ram Das and the other guests ran after him. But when they reached the spot, they were surprised to see Kabir lovingly embracing the buffalo saying, "Oh my Lord, today you have received such bad injuries, which you had not received even with your battles with the demon Ravana, or your battle with Kamsa. Oh Lord, seeing you in this condition pains me very deeply..."

Suddenly, seeing Kabir weeping in this way for the buffalo brought a change of heart over everyone present. As if by a miracle, they too began to see God in the form of this buffalo. Soon their hearts seemed to melt with pity and love for the poor creature. For a moment they too had the vision of unity consciousness, and like Kabir, for a few moments they were able to perceive God in all things.

Muhammad and the Old Woman

Although many people accepted the teachings of Muhammad, not everyone did so. He was often abused and insulted by unbelievers, but he never felt any hatred or anger towards such people. On the contrary, a story is related that whenever he used to pass by a certain house in Mecca, an old woman would throw garbage on his head from her window.

Muhammad never said anything and would just continue on his way. Now it so happened that for a few days no garbage was thrown on him when he passed the house. Surprised at this, he made some inquires and found out that the woman had been ill for a few days. Upon hearing this, Muhammad immediately went to the woman's home and started to care for her. When she saw Muhammad, the woman became ashamed of her past actions and apologized to the prophet. And shortly after she became his follower.

Heaven and Hell

There was once a great Guru who was known for his mystical powers. One day a seeker approached him and asked what was heaven like. "Can you show me heaven?" he asked.

"Yes I can," answered the Guru, "but only with the condition that we first visit hell."

The seeker agreed and the Guru told him to sit in meditation. The Guru then placed his hand on the seeker's head, and suddenly they were both moving about in their subtle bodies. They soon reached the hellish regions, where it happened to be lunch time. The lunch bell was rung, calling all the residents of hell to the meal. When the residents arrived, they all sat in front of what looked like a wonderful feast. There were all types of delicious dishes. There was steaming rice, beautiful cooked vegetables, pastas, pizza, cakes, and ice cream.

The seeker thought, "Even in hell there appears to be delicious food." But although there were many wonderful dishes on the table, the residents all looked famished, as if they had not eaten in a long time. This surprised the seeker, but the reason would soon become apparent. Before the meal started, the demon guards strapped a long wooden spoon to the right arm of each of the residents. The problem with this was that although they could scoop up the food, the spoons were so long, they could not bend their arms; it was impossible to get any of the food into their mouths. This created nothing but turmoil, and everyone just cursed their inability to get even a kernel of rice into their mouths. When seeing this sad condition, the seeker realized how much these poor souls were suffering.

"Now let us go to heaven," said the Guru.

Immediately they were in heaven, where it was also lunch time. The seeker could see that the same kinds of delicious dishes were on the table. He noticed that the same types of spoons were strapped to the right arms of the residents. However, everyone looked healthy and well fed. And, instead of curses, he noticed that they were all joking and laughing with each other. This surprised the seeker and he asked the Guru why they were so happy, since the conditions appeared to be similar to those in hell.

But the moment they started eating, the seeker saw a most wonderful thing. Although they could not feed themselves, they had learned that by simply feeding the person to their left with their spoons, they were all able to feed each other.

In the same way, this world is both heaven and hell. As long as we don't respect and cooperate with each other, we simply can't experience any happiness. But the moment we learn cooperation and help each other, we experience joy and become fulfilled.

The Merchant and the Thief

Not long after Birbal entered the services of the Moghul Emperor Akbar, two men appeared in the great hall before the king. One was an honest merchant, but the other was nothing but a thief.

Although both men were wealthy, the thief had made his fortune by cheating other rich people. He had devised a clever plan for defrauding them. He would first become friends with the person posing as an honest and good man. When he had finally won their confidence, he would swindle them out of their wealth. He was so successful that up to then he had never been caught.

The two men were now before the king, with the cheat claiming that the merchant had robbed him. In fact, what had occurred was that the scoundrel had befriended the merchant, and after winning his confidence invited him to his home for a lavish dinner.

Not suspecting anything, the merchant went alone. When he arrived at the thief's home, he noticed that a number of the thief's friends were also there. Since there was plenty to eat and drink, everyone was enjoying themselves. After the dinner was over, the merchant went home apparently pleased with the events of the evening.

However, the next morning, the merchant was surprised when the thief suddenly showed up at his door accusing him of stealing a precious diamond. The merchant assured the man that he was mistaken, but the scoundrel just ignored him. The thief insisted on the return of the diamond or else payment for it.

As the merchant refused to pay, the cheat took the matter to Akbar. He also brought three friends who had been at the dinner as his eyewitnesses. All three said that the merchant had stolen the diamond.

Akbar listened to both sides of the story and had the feeling the merchant was honest, but in the end, he could not tell who he should believe. Then, noticing Birbal standing nearby he asked, "Birbal, as you have heard both sides of the story, can you tell which one is guilty in this matter?"

"I will try, Your Majesty," answered Birbal. Then for a moment Birbal became thoughtful. After a few minutes he asked for some clay to be brought. He divided it into three pieces and gave one to each witness saying, "Since all three of you have seen the diamond which was stolen by the merchant, I want each of you to shape the clay according to your memory of the diamond."

Saying this, he directed them into three separate rooms. Finding themselves alone in those rooms, the three witnesses did not know what to do, as in fact none had ever seen any diamond.

Now it so happened that each belonged to a different profession. One was a tailor, the second a barber, and the third a carpenter. As the tailor wondered what to do, he recalled his mother telling him that his needle was as valuable to him as a diamond. He therefore decided to shape the clay in the form of a needle. Meanwhile, the barber had recalled what his father had told him, that his razor was as precious to him as a diamond. So he shaped the clay like a razor. The carpenter remembered his teachers instruction, to guard his saw as he would a diamond, so he shaped the clay like a saw.

When they were finished, they were brought once again before Akbar. Seeing the strange shapes which they made, Birbal said, "It is clear, Your Majesty, that these men have never seen a diamond."

"You are right," answered the king, "it is now clear who is lying." So he immediately ordered his men to arrest the thief and throw him into prison.

Birbal was highly praised, and from that day onwards, the king began seeking his guidance more often. And Birbal's fame as a wise man also began to grow.

The Man Who Played
The Plow-Harp

In India, during the period of the Mughals, the monarchy would often entertain musicians and artists. They would also reward the artists lavishly.

Now at that time, there was a poor farmer who could barely support his family. He had heard of the king's generous offer to the musicians and although not musically inclined himself, he tried to think of a way to take advantage of this opportunity.

One day, he suddenly came upon a plan and picked up his plow which he used for the fields. He tied it up in a sheet and holding it under his arm, he headed towards the court. There he attached himself to a band of musicians waiting for their turn to perform for the emperor Akbar.

Soon it was the group's turn and they all sat down ready to perform. The farmer sat with them holding his plow instrument. When the group started playing, the farmer also made different hand gestures with his plow, as if playing it.

Soon the king noticed the man and the unusual instrument he was playing. After the musicians played for sometime, the king asked the farmer, "What kind of instrument is that you are playing? I have never seen anything like it before."

The farmer replied, "It is called the *halva*, the plow harp, and I am an expert on it."

"Will you kindly play something on it for me," requested the king.

"O no your majesty," answered the farmer sadly, "this instrument can not be played alone, but can only be played in a group with other instruments."

My Guru used to love this story and would often tell it when trying to encourage everyone to participate in the chants. He would say, "Don't sit silently pretending to play your plow instrument."

The Palace of Mirrors

Once during a carnival, a man went into the palace of mirrors. Everywhere he looked, he saw his own reflection. If he looked to the side, there were more images of himself, if he looked behind, there also more images of him. He saw many reflections of himself, but they were all a little different from each other, and they changed as he moved or tilted his head slightly. Some of the images made him look thin, while others fat, and still others tall or short.

He became so excited at seeing so many images of himself that he had to sit down. "How wonderful this place is?" he thought to himself, "There are so many reflections of me." The man left the palace of mirrors feeling happy.

Meanwhile, a dog had wandered into the palace of mirrors. As the dog rushed about, he saw many other dogs coming at him from the opposite direction. He would turn to run away, but wherever he turned, he saw more dogs charging at him. The unfortunate dog became terrified.

Alone and surrounded by so many apparent enemies, the dog began barking ferociously and started jumping in the air trying to escape. Then suddenly, filled with so much fear and rage, the poor dog collapsed on the spot.

In the same way, this universe is like the palace of mirrors. It is the dance or play of creation which vibrates and is modified into innumerable forms and shapes. One who is liberated perceives this dance and is not bothered by it. But one who sees the many reflections as so many enemies, as the dog saw them, they will always experience only misery.

The Miserly King

There was once a king who was so stingy that he was
called the Miserly King by everyone. It so happened
that one day, an acting couple came to the kingdom
to perform a play. For several days, the husband and wife
performed for the king and his courtiers, but the king had as
yet not given them a single penny. It was customary that the
king should at least have given them something.

The poor actor and his wife were now out of money and could
hardly get food for themselves, but they continued with their
performance. One night, before they started, they announced
that it would be their last performance. Perhaps hoping to
remind the stingy king to give them something.

After the announcement, the actors started to perform with
great enthusiasm. The play was very long, but when they saw
that it was already 2 a.m., and the king had still not given
anything, the wife lost all hope and started to slacken in her
performance. When the actor saw this, he recited a verse hoping
to encourage her, saying, "A long time has passed already, there
is not much time left. So don't slacken now, only a few more
hours, and we will be done."

An ascetic, who was sitting in the audience when he heard
the actor's verse, picked up his old blanket and threw it to
the actor. Then, the princess, who was also in the audience,

removed her valuable necklace and threw it towards the actor as well. The prince, who was sitting next to his sister, removed a beautiful emerald ring from his finger and tossed it on stage to the couple.

Before long the play was over. However, the king was enraged that his son and daughter gave such valuable gifts to the couple. Even though he himself had not given them anything, he could not bear anyone else giving anything either. But he was curious, and called out to the ascetic and asked, "Babaji, you had only one blanket, what made you give it to the actor?"

"Your Majesty," answered the ascetic, "when I arrived here and saw the splendor of your palace, it made me reflect on my own life. I have spent many years living as an ascetic, fasting, and remaining a celibate for so many years, but I have still not reached my goal. So when I saw your beautiful palace, I decided to give up my practices and change my life so that one day, I too could become a king like you and enjoy all types of pleasures and power."

"But at that moment," continued the ascetic, "I heard the actor's words, 'A long time has passed already, there is not much time left. So don't slacken now, only a few more hours and we will be done,' and suddenly, I realized that most of my life has already passed living this way of life. Now that there is only a short time left, what point would there be to change my way of life? This realization made me so happy that I threw my only blanket to him in sheer gratitude."

The king then asked his daughter why she threw her valuable necklace to the actors. "Father," the princess said, "as you know,

I am old enough to marry. But still, because you are so miserly, you have not bothered to think about a husband for me. So I had decided to elope with the son of a rich man. But then I heard the actor's verse, and I thought, 'I have already waited for so many years. You are now an old man and will probably die soon. So why should I elope and spoil our families good name?' Out of gratitude, I threw my necklace to the actor."

Then turning to his son, the king asked, "And why did you throw your ring to the actor?"

"When a son comes of age," the prince replied, "his father should turn over the throne to his son and go into the forest to perform austerities. That is our custom. But you are so greedy that you continue to hold on to power, probably until the end of your life. I have therefore lately been thinking of ways to dispose of you. But then I heard the actor's words. So I thought, 'So much time has already passed. You are old and will probably not live much longer. So why should I commit such a heinous crime as murdering my own father?' So in gratitude I threw my ring to the actor."

Although only one verse was spoken, three listeners understood it in different ways. Each according to their own situation. This story is told in the Yoga Vasishtha in order to illustrate how we see our own projections in the world and respond to them differently.

I Could Have Been Killed!

One night, thinking he had heard a strange noise outside in his garden, Nasrudin got out of bed to investigate. He went to the window and looked out. In the dim moonlight, he thought he saw a figure dressed in a white *kaftan* — a long sleeved garment reaching the ankles — in the distance. There were clouds in the sky that night and the moon appeared to dart in and out from behind them. The wind was blowing and he could hear what he was sure was the flapping of a thief's garments.

"Who goes there?" shouted Nasrudin.

Hearing no reply, Nasrudin called to his wife to hand him his bow and arrows.

"What are you going to do?" asked his anxious wife.

"I am going to shoot that prowler," Nasrudin replied.

"Go away, thief," shouted Nasrudin. But the figure did not move.

"Leave now or I will shoot you with my bow and arrow," he again shouted. But there was no response.

"I am placing the arrow on my bow," yelled Nasrudin. Still the figure stood there.

"I am now pulling back the bowstring," warned the Mullah.

He wanted to give the thief every opportunity to flee. For shooting a man was of course the last thing Nasrudin wanted to do. Finally, he decided to fire a warning shot in the general direction of the thief, thereby making good on his threat but at the same time missing the fellow.

"There," shouted Nasrudin, thinking that the intruder had run away. "Now let us go back to bed," he said to his wife Fatima.

The next morning Nasrudin went out to investigate, only to discover that he had shot his own kaftan which was hanging on the close line drying. Seeing this he let out a loud cry and began shouting, "Thank God! Thank God! That was a close call."

"What are you thanking God for," shouted his wife as she came running out to see what the commotion was about.

"Thank God! Thank God!" Nasrudin kept shouting, "For as you can see, my dear wife, the arrow pierced right through the heart of my kaftan. And if I were in it, I would certainly be dead now."

The Portrait

There was a Roman painter who decided to paint a portrait which represented an ideal youth. He wanted for his subject a young man who had all the best qualities of a human being. He wanted someone who had the vitality and strength of youth — someone who was virtuous and intelligent.

The painter traveled from town to town and village to village in search of such a person. Finally, in a small town he came across a handsome boy, whom he thought was an ideal subject. When he inquired about the boy, he learned that he came from a good family and had some talent. Thinking he had found his subject, the painter made an exact portrait of the boy.

Soon the painting became very popular. The government even had copies made and had them placed at different parts of the towns and cities. They were placed at schools, churches, and prisons, hoping that it would inspire others to become the best they could be.

After some years had passed, that same artist thought of painting a portrait which would reflect the opposite of the earlier portrait of the youth. He was now looking for a person who exemplified brutality, wickedness, and the most vile qualities of humankind. He wanted someone who could steal, and even murder without giving it a second thought. But although the painter visited many cities and towns looking for such a cruel character, he could not find anyone to his liking. One day, he decided to look in the prisons hoping to find such an evil person. There he found one man who seemed to fit his artistic vision exactly. Even the man's hideous face appeared to express his cruel nature.

So, the painter immediately started his portrait. When he was finished, it appeared that he had captured the very depths of the man's heartless nature. Soon copies of this portrait were also made and hung all over the city alongside the first portrait. Copies were also placed at all the prisons as well.

Finally, the day arrived when the prisoner who had posed for the painting was released from prison. When he walked out of the prison cell to the outside world, he noticed the two portraits hanging along side each other. The moment he saw them tears started rolling down his cheeks, and he started crying like a child. Soon a crowd gathered around him. They tried to pacify him asking why he was crying. Since he was just released from prison they thought he should be happy. "What is the matter?" they asked. "Why are you crying?"

"When I looked at those two portraits," said the man, "I couldn't help but cry."

"But why?" someone asked.

"Because both portraits are of me," answered the man sadly. "You see, I was once like that first portrait. I came from a good family and was happy with life. But then I started keeping the wrong company, and as a result, I have become what is represented in the second portrait. When I look at these two portraits, I cannot help but cry."

"In this body," my Guru would often say, "anything can be done." The Bhagavad Gita calls this body a field, indicating that life's conditions are created by the type of seeds we ourselves sow. How can one experience happiness and peace if we sow jealously and hatred? Therefore, we should sow only good qualities.

A Disciple's Love

Early in the 14th century, Amir Khusrau was the court poet of the Delhi ruler Alauddin, and afterwards became Ghiasuddin Tughlaq's court poet. He was also extremely attached to his Guru, Sheikh Nizamuddin Aulia, who also lived in Delhi.

Now it so happened that when Nizamuddin died, Amir Khusrau was in Bengal where he had accompanied Sultan Ghiasuddin Tughlaq. Some say that it was Nizamuddin himself who had suggested that he go. Knowing that his disciple would be overwhelmed by his death, Nizamuddin told some of his close followers that when Amir Khusrau returned, he should not be told immediately where his tomb was.

However, when Amir Khusrau returned to Delhi and heard of Nizamuddin's death, he discovered where his Guru had been buried and immediately ran to his tomb. While still at some distance, he saw the holy shrine. Amir Khusrau became overwhelmed with sorrow and uttered the following poem:

> A maiden is sleeping on her bed,
> Her face is covered with her hair.
> Oh Khusrau, go back home,
> Dusk is falling all around.

While repeating this poem, it is said that out of love for his Guru,

Amir Khusrau suddenly breathed his last, collapsing on the spot. He was buried next to his beloved Guru. Today both Hindus and Muslims pay homage to them. Their combined mausoleum was one of my Guru's favorite places of pilgrimage, which he had visited a number of times.

Who Can Make This Line Shorter?

Birbal was a wise counselor in the court of the great Moghul emperor, Akbar. He was very clever and often delighted the king with his quick wit. One day, Akbar drew a line on the ground outside the courtyard. "Who can make this line shorter?" asked the king of his courtiers. "Without, however, erasing or touching the original line in any way," he added.

Everyone was puzzled by this proposal. But Birbal stood up and walked over to where the line was drawn and quickly drew a second but longer line. Everyone, including the king, was delighted at the result. Birbal had indeed succeeded in shorting the first line without erasing or even touching it.

Swami Ram Tirtha used to pose this problem to his own students. We too should succeed in life and prosper, without harming or showing disrespect to others. We should not think that we have to tear down or be always in competition with others to achieve our goals. It can be done by simply putting forth our best efforts.

The Greatness of God's Name

There was once a saintly woman who lived in her Guru's ashram. She, like her Guru, enjoyed chanting God's holy names. As a service to the ashram, she would prepare cow-dung chips which in India are used for fuel. She would spread them out so they could be dried by the sun. Now a neighbor would do the same thing, but one day the chips happened to get mixed up, and the neighbor claimed even the disciple's cakes as her own.

When the Guru heard of the disagreement, he said that he would be able to pick out the cakes belonging to his disciple without any trouble and immediately began to pick up each cake and held it to his ear. He would then say, "This one is hers, this one is not, this one is hers, this one is not..."

Soon there were two piles, one he said belonged to his disciple, and the other to the neighbor. Curious as to how the Guru was able to discover which were really hers and which were those of his disciple, the neighbor asked him how he did it.

"It is easy," the Guru replied, "as I held each patty to my ear, I could hear the name of God being repeated in the patties prepared by my disciple, because she repeats God's sacred Name while performing all of her work. Because of this, the vibration created by the Name was absorbed by the cakes, and so, I was able to hear it."

Chanting God's Name has such power that even inanimate objects are influenced by it. My own Guru related his personal experience of this truth by an incident which occurred during his early days as a wandering monk. He had heard of a great saint who was considered an authority on the mantra, "Om Namah Shivaya." Having an interest in this mantra, my Guru went to the saint's ashram. After bowing to the saint, he asked him to give him some instructions on the mantra. The saint did not answer directly but instead asked him to pick up one of his shoes which were placed near his seat and hold it up to his ear. When he did so, to his surprise he began hearing, "Om Namah Shivaya! Om Namah Shivaya! Om Namah Shivaya!" coming from the shoe. He looked at the saint with astonishment. The saint told him that one should repeat the mantra with such intensity that every drop of his blood should contain the mantra; every fiber of cloth he wore should be permeated with the mantra; and that every object he touched should repeat this mantra.

How Many Gods Are There?

Once the great sage Yajnavalkya was answering questions in the court of king Janaka. "How many gods are there, O Yajnavalkya?" asked one of those gathered named Vidagdha.

Thinking of the traditional list of cosmic deities, Yajnavalkya replied, "3306."

"Yes," said Vidagdha, "but how many gods are there really?"

"Thirty-three," answered Yajnavalkya.

"Yes, but how many are there really?" again asked Vidagdha.

"Six," replied Yajnavalkya.

"Tell me truly, Yajnavalkya, how many gods are there?" Vidagdha pleaded.

"Three," said Yajnavalkya.

"Yes, but exactly how many gods are there Yajnavalkya?" Vidagdha persisted.

"One," answered Yajnavalkya.

The Vedas have said, "Truly, God is One — there can be no second. He alone governs these worlds with His powers. He stands facing beings. He, the herdsman, after bringing forth all worlds, reabsorbs them at the end of Time."

The Buddha's Lineage

Once, Lord Buddha happened to be visiting his father's capital. When it was time for his meals, Buddha, as is the custom of mendicants, approached a few houses for alms. A monk usually does not ask for anything but simply stands in front of a house. If he gets something to eat fine, but if he does not, then he will not eat that day.

His father, who was a *raja* — a king, came to know that his son was in the city and wished to see him. The Buddha, who previously was a prince, had left his father's palace at the age of 29 to lead a mendicant's life and so his father had not seen him for many years.

When his father arrived and saw his son dressed in the garb of a *sannyasin* (mendicant) begging for his food, the king was sad and shed bitter tears. He approached the Buddha and said, "Son, dear prince, I never did this, I never took up the garb of a mendicant, my father, your grandfather, never lived the life of a mendicant and wandered throughout the streets. We have been kings, you belong to a royal family. This day you are bringing disgrace and shame to the whole family. Please keep my honor and give up this way of life."

Buddha listened quietly to the king's words, and smiling he said, "Sir, please listen carefully. By practice of deep meditation, I have seen my family lineage. I have looked to my previous birth and the one before that, and I see that the family to which I belong has been a family of mendicants all along."

To illustrate his meaning, the Buddha continued by saying, "Oh King, from your previous births you have been coming from the line of kings, while I have been coming from this line, and in this birth we have met, as if at the crossing of two roads. Now I have to go my way, and you must go yours."

The Price of a Slap

One day, Mullah Nasrudin was walking in the marketplace when all of a sudden a total stranger walked up behind him and slapped him on the back of his head. When Nasrudin turned around, he saw a man he had never seen before.

"How dare you slap me!" shouted the Mullah furiously.

"Oh, I beg your pardon," said the man, "I thought you were someone else."

But Nasrudin was not satisfied with this explanation, and he brought the stranger before the local magistrate demanding compensation.

However, Nasrudin quickly perceived that the magistrate and the stranger were friends. The latter admitted his guilt, and the judge pronounced the sentence: "The settlement for this offense is one dollar, which is to be paid to the plaintiff. However, if you do not have a dollar with you," the judge added, "then you may bring it here to the plaintiff at your convenience."

The defendant went on his way upon hearing the sentence. Nasrudin waited for the man to return with his payment. But after waiting for almost three hours, Nasrudin said to the magistrate, "Do I understand correctly that one dollar is sufficient payment for a slap?"

"Yes," answered the magistrate.

Hearing the answer, Nasrudin slapped the magistrate in the face and said, "In that case, you may keep my dollar when the defendant returns with it." And with that, the Mullah went on his way.

Alexander and the Sadhus

It is said that when Alexander left Macedonia for Persia, and then India, he asked his teacher Aristotle if he wished him to bring anything special back from India. As the Greeks considered India a place of deep spirituality and the land of *yoga*, Aristotle told Alexander, "If you can manage, bring back a great *yogi*."

So once, during Alexander's campaign in India, he came across some holy men (*sadhus*) who were sitting near a river discussing philosophy. On seeing Alexander, the sadhus all began stomping their feet on the ground. Surprised at this action, Alexander inquired through interpreters on its meaning. One of the holy men replied, "O king Alexander, each man possesses no more of this earth than the patch we stand on; yet you, though a man like other men, except of course that you are restless and presumptuous are roaming over so wide an area away from what is your own giving no rest to yourself or others. Very soon you too will die and will possess no more of the earth than suffices for the burial of your body."

On another occasion, Alexander had heard of a group of naked sadhus living near the famous city of Taxila. He came to admire them and wished that one of them would accompany him back to Macedonia. He therefore approached the Guru of the group and made his request. But the Guru turned down his request. He said that like Alexander, he too was a great emperor, and therefore had no need of anything Alexander could give him. He was completely contented with what he had.

Alexander was disappointed but he eventually did find a sadhu who accompanied him back to Persia. His name was Kalyan, but that is another story...

How Akbar and Birbal Met

O f all the Moghul rulers of India, Akbar was without doubt the greatest. Born in 1542 C.E., in the Sind providence of modern day Pakistan, Akbar succeeded to his father's throne when he was only thirteen years of age. But during the years of his father's exile in Persia, Akbar was brought up among the tough Afghanistani warriors and is said to have had great courage.

Although he remained illiterate throughout his life, in contrast to his highly educated father and grandfather, he would surpass them with his intellectual capacity. He was generous to his subjects and was particularly tolerant of religious beliefs. This could not be said of all his ancestors. He loved wisdom and would invite leaders of all religions to the palace hall for discussions and debates.

Now when the king was younger, he loved to hunt. One day he and his friends went to a certain forest to hunt. They had been told that there were many wild animals there. But as it turned out, although they wandered far, they found no animals. It was a hot day, and they soon became very thirsty. They decided to look for a stream or pond where they could drink some water but unfortunately they found none.

"We must find a village," suggested one of the men. Akbar agreed and they set off in search of one. After riding for sometime, they came across a young boy about the age of ten. As Akbar drew closer, he called out to the boy asking if there was a village nearby.

"Yes Sir," answered the boy politely, "my village is not far from here. We have a well which contains plenty of water."

"Then please take us there," said Akbar.

The boy eagerly agreed and one of the horsemen pulled him up onto the back of his horse, and they rode off in the direction shown by the boy. Before long, they reached the village and the boy drew some water for them. He filled a jug and poured water for each one of them. When the boy came before Akbar, the young king gave the boy a closer look. He thought the boy to be quite bright and asked, "What is your name?"

"Tell me first what your name is?" the boy quickly shot back boldly.

Akbar was surprised, since he was not used to people speaking to him in that manner. "Do you know who I am?" demanded the king angrily.

"Do you know who I am?" the boy replied with a smile.

This time Akbar burst out laughing. He had a good sense of humor and he was starting to like the straight forwardness of the young boy. Slipping off a large emerald ring from his finger, he handed it to the boy.

The moment the boy saw the ring, he was stunned, for he now

knew who he was speaking to. For although he was young, he immediately recognized the royal seal on the ring. The boy was so surprised that he literally could not speak.

Akbar was quite amused to see the boy's response, but he said, "When you get older, come and visit me at my palace in Agra. And bring this ring with you so that I will recognize you."

So saying, the king and his men rode off leaving the young boy behind pondering everything that had occurred. He also examined the ring more carefully. When the king and his men rode off, the boy ran home. He immediately showed his widowed mother the precious ring and related exactly what had occurred. His mother became very happy when she heard that her son had met the king but became upset when he told her what he had said to him.

"You should have been more polite and told him that your name is Mahesh Das," his mother said in a scolding voice. But the next moment she smiled at the boy and was happy to think of the wonderful future opportunities serving the king would bring him. Like every mother, she hoped for a bright future for her child. She said to her son, "Mahesh, you are a clever and intelligent boy, but you must study hard in order to be of service to the king."

"Yes mother," agreed Mahesh. "I will then take this ring to the king, and he will know me."

"Very good!" smiled the mother. "But perhaps you better give me the ring for safe keeping. If you were to lose it, the king might not remember you."

Obediently the boy handed the ring to his mother. As time passed, Mahesh would sometimes even forget he had the ring, but he continued to study hard and became learned and wise.

Finally, by the time he completed his studies he had grown into an intelligent young man. His mother decided it was now time for him to visit Akbar at his court.

"My son," said the old woman, "you are now grown up and so it is time for you to go to Agra and meet Akbar, the king. She went and got the ring and handed it to Mahesh. Although he was sad to leave his old mother, Mahesh readily agreed to go. This would be a new adventure for him, and he was looking forward to seeing the great city of Agra.

After a long and tiring journey, Mahesh reached Agra. He walked through the narrow lanes of the city and being stimulated by all the sights and sounds, his weariness soon left him. Having never seen such a sight, he could only stare in wonder at the bustling activity of the city.

At last, he reached the palace gates and asked the guard on duty to allow him to enter. But the guard refused. "Why?" asked Mahesh in surprise. "Everyone knows that the king meets his subjects quite freely," he said. "You cannot stop me from entering."

"I can stop you!" the guard answered rudely. "I decide who can enter and who can not." But he then added in a low voice, "But I will let you in if you give me something."

"You mean I must pay you in order to get in?" asked Mahesh in amazement. He could not believe the man's dishonesty.

"I have no money," answered Mahesh. But he suddenly got an idea and said, "But if you allow me to meet the king, who knows, he may reward me in some way, and then I can pay you something."

"All right!" agreed the dishonest guard. "I will let you in, but you better give me half of whatever the king gives you as a gift."

"Agreed," Mahesh said. "You will get half of whatever the king gives me."

The guard opened the gate and Mahesh went in. As he walked through the palace gardens, young Mahesh was amazed at the exquisite landscaping. He had never seen anything so beautiful in his life. There were fountains everywhere and flowers of all colors blooming in the gardens.

As beautiful as the gardens were, the palace itself was exquisitely designed, with its numerous minarets and great domes. There were beautifully carved pillars with domed ceilings covered with tiny pieces of glass organized into various patterns. The marble floors were so smooth and spotless that one could see their own reflection in them. Mahesh marveled at all he saw. He thought he was dreaming and had gone to heaven never imagining how grand the king's palace could be.

The throne room was even more spectacular. The large hall radiated grandeur with all its royal curtains and beautifully rich carpets. At the far end of the room, on a golden throne, studded with precious stones, sat Emperor Akbar. The king was dressed in a blue satin shirt and a golden silk turban. He wore a diamond necklace and a number of rings made from precious stones sparkled on his fingers.

In all this splendor, Mahesh became a little nervous. After all, it had been a number of years since he had first met Akbar. But he quickly regained his composure and joined the crowd of courtiers who were waiting for a chance to speak to the king. When the opportunity arose, Mahesh took out the ring which Akbar had given him.

"Your Majesty," Mahesh said, "do you recognize this ring?"

"Of course I recognize the ring," Akbar replied, "and I also recognize you too. You are that little boy whom I met years ago. I am happy to see you again."

The king invited the young man to sit near him, and he inquired as to all that had happened since they first met. After speaking to Mahesh for some time, Akbar saw that Mahesh was an intelligent young man and also sensed a certain wisdom in him. Pleased with the young man, the king said, "Tell me what I can do for you. Ask for anything and I will grant it."

"Your Majesty, you are very kind," answered Mahesh humbly. "If you wish to grant me something, then kindly order your guards to give me fifty lashes of the whip."

"Fifty lashes of the whip?" the king shouted in surprise. "That is what you want?"

In fact, everyone in the hall was astonished at the strange

request. "Yes indeed," answered Mahesh, "fifty lashes of the whip is what I desire."

"But how can I grant such a request?" Akbar asked. "That would be a terrible punishment, and you have done nothing wrong."

"I assure you, Your Majesty," Mahesh insisted, "I will consider fifty lashes not as a punishment, but a great gift."

When he saw that Mahesh was determined, Akbar started rethinking his assessment of the young man. He was now convinced that Mahesh was a bit mad, and wondered how he could have considered him as a wise man. Nevertheless, he finally agreed, but said, "Before we grant this strange request of yours, you must tell us the reason why."

Mahesh bowed to the king in obedience, and related his earlier encounter with the guard at the front gate. He said, "When I arrived at the palace gates, the guard on duty allowed me to enter, but only with the condition that I share with him half of whatever I received from you as a gift. I am therefore ready to bear twenty-five lashes in order to share them with the guard who rightfully deserves the remaining lashes."

Akbar was surprised to hear of the guard's dishonesty. But at the same time he understood the reason for Mahesh's strange request. Seeing Mahesh's cleverness, the king laughed, but immediately ordered that the guard be brought before him.

The guard wondered why he was being summoned by the king, but when he saw Mahesh speaking to the Emperor, he became afraid. "Have our people been kept away by a greedy and wicked guard?" shouted the king in anger. He then told the guard, "As fifty lashes were requested, you yourself will receive the entire gift."

When the guard heard what was to be his share of Mahesh's gift, he could hardly believe his ears. He began to beg for forgiveness, but Akbar refused. He in fact ordered that the punishment be given right then and there.

After this was over, the king said to the guard, "I hope you have learned your lesson. From now on, allow everyone to enter my court freely."

He then turned to Mahesh, and with a smile said, "You are truly a wise man Mahesh. I have therefore decided to bestow on you the title of *Birbal*, meaning 'one who is wise.' From this day onwards, you will stay here at the palace and guide us."

And so began the long and beautiful friendship between Akbar and Birbal. With his wisdom and wit, Birbal would guide the king and also bring humor and good cheer to his court.

God Is Very Close

When the divine is not understood, it appears far from us. But when understood, it is very near to us. To illustrate this point the following story is told.

There was once a girl of marriageable age and her parents made arrangements to find a groom. They found what they thought was a suitable boy, however, the girl was determined to marry a person who was the best and highest among all else. Seeing her determination, her parents left her alone.

The young girl started thinking about who she wanted to marry and concluded that the king of the land was higher than everyone else, and she therefore decided that she would marry only him and began following him.

Now one day, the king was riding in a palanquin, when he happened to meet a *sadhu*, a holy man. The king got down and made his obeisance to the mendicant and then continued on his way. Seeing this the girl thought, "What a fool I have been, thinking that the king is the highest among men. The *sannyasi* appears to be higher even than the king. I must somehow marry the holy man."

Thinking this way, the girl started following the *sannyasi*. Then one day, while following the monk, she saw him paying respects to a *lingam* — an image of Lord Shiva in the shape of an oval stone — which was placed under a Banyan tree. She then changed her opinion and decided to marry Lord Shiva, as she found him to be even higher than the holy man who had paid homage to him.

Instead of following the sadhu, she now sat near the tree close to the image. This was not a temple but a natural setting and not many people passed that way. One day, as she sat gazing on the image, a dog passing by suddenly relieved himself on the *lingam*. Upon witnessing this, the poor young girl thought that the dog must be higher than even Shiva, and so she started running after him.

She followed the dog, and soon they were in a local market. The dog started sniffing near a shop, when suddenly the shopkeeper struck him with a stick. The dog started howling in pain and ran off. A young man who was watching this yelled at the shopkeeper and chastised him for being unkind to the poor creature who had after all done him no harm. When seeing this, the young girl thought that this person who had chastised the shopkeeper must be the best person and decided to marry him alone. As it turned out, that young man was the one who had originally been chosen by her parents. Therefore, the person whom she thought was far from her was in fact very close.

In the same way, we are always searching for God as though He were far away from us. And as long as He is not known, He appears to be at a great distance from us. But the moment we realize Him, His intimacy is revealed.

The Churning of the Cosmic Ocean

A t one time, eons ago, the *Asuras* (demons) became very powerful. When any of them were slain by the beings of light (*Devas*) they would be revived by their Guru, Sukracharya. He had obtained the knowledge of *Sanjivan*, the ability of bringing the dead back to life. The Devas became frightened since the *Asura* population was becoming larger while theirs was dwindling. Therefore they approached Brahma the creator for guidance. He advised them to approach Narayana, the Supreme Lord who sleeps on the cosmic ocean. The Devas propitiated Narayana and asked him to guide them. Lord Narayana instructed them to churn the cosmic ocean for the divine nectar (*amrita*) hidden within it. He told them that whosoever drank it would become immune to death.

However, he also told them that they would require the help of the *Asuras* to fulfill such a difficult task and that they should therefore cultivate a friendship with them for that purpose.

Following the Lord's advice, the *Devas* approached the *Asuras* with the proposition, and they agreed to work together. They decided to use the Mandara mountain as the churning rod, and the cosmic serpent Ananta-Shesha as the rope. But they found that they could not move the mountain, and so Lord Vishnu (Narayana) had to assist them. The gods were afraid of the serpent's many mouths, so they decided they would rather take hold of the tale. But the demons were bold, and they quickly grabbed a hold of the different heads of the serpent. Obviously they lost a few demons in the process, but having a strong desire for the nectar, they held on.

But even after a long time of churning nothing was produced. They began to feel tired and became dejected thinking that the task was an impossible one. Seeing their gloomy faces, Lord Vishnu decided to once again help them and inspired them to continue. As soon as the churning started up again in earnest, the deadly poison called *kalakuta* appeared on the surface of the ocean and started killing both the gods and demons.

The survivors ran to Shiva, the death conquering Lord (*Mrityunjaya*), and brought him to the sea. After pleasing him with their hymns, he collected the poison and started drinking it. But remembering that the Lord dwelt in his heart, he decided to keep the poison in his throat which turned blue. This is why he later came to be known as *Neelakantha*, the blue throated Lord.

The churning started up again, but this time the mountain started sinking into the sea. Again Lord Vishnu came to their rescue by transforming himself into *Kurma*, the cosmic tortoise and held the mountain on his back. This gave the gods and demons encouragement, and the churning became faster.

The churning rod moved back and forth, back and forth, but this time the results were good. Soon all types of treasures started to arise from the sea. *Kamadhenu*, the wish fulfilling cow arose, along with the Elephant *Airavata*, and the white horse *Uchchalhrava*. Precious gems, as well as the wish fulfilling tree, the *Kalpa-Vriksha,* also arose. The beautiful *Apsara*, Urvashi arose, as well as the Goddess Lakshmi.

The gods and demons divided all these treasures between themselves leaving only the Goddess Lakshmi. Later a dispute arose between them for the hand of Lakshmi, and they both tried to win her over. However, after finding one fault or another with all her suitors, she chose Lord Vishnu. Surya, the Sun god, took the white horse *Uchchalhrava*, and Indra, the lord of the gods, took the Elephant *Airavata*.

After the dispute was over, the churning started again and a beautiful girl named *Sura*—the goddess of wine—arose. The demons immediately claimed her, and the gods did not object.

As the churning continued, a being named Dhanvantari appeared holding the pot of nectar. As soon as the demons saw him, they snatched the pot from his hands and a general fight broke out. Indra, the leader of the *Devas* saw this and sent his son Jayanta to recapture the precious nectar. Jayanta transformed himself into a bird and flew down on the demons and grabbing the pot flew off with it upwards, towards the heavens. The demons began chasing him, and the gods followed close behind.

It is said that the chase lasted for twelve celestial days, which is equal to twelve human years. In the process, Jayanta had to rest because of fatigue, and he laid the pot down at four different places in India. These are: on the banks of the river Godavari in Nashik; on the banks of the river Shipra in Ujjain; on the banks of the river Ganga at Haridwar, located at the foothills of the Himalayas; and at the *Sangam* or confluence of the three rivers Ganga, Yamuna, and Sarasvati at Prayaga—modern Allahabad.

During those stops, the Sun, Moon, Jupiter, and Saturn stood guard over the pot (*kumbha*). Even so, a few drops of the nectar is said to have fallen into the waters of the rivers at these four places.

It is for this reason that *sadhus* gather at these places for a holy bath when the Sun, Moon, and the planet Jupiter are in certain constellations. This event came to be called the *Kumbha-Mela* and is timed by Jupiter's cycle. The planet Jupiter takes approximately twelve years to complete one cycle through all twelve constellations. When he is in the constellation of Leo and the Sun and Moon are in Aries, the mela is held at Ujjain. When the three are located in Leo, it is held at Nashik on the banks of the river Godavari. When the Sun and Moon are in Aries and Jupiter is in Aquarius, it is held in Haridwar. And when Jupiter is in Taurus, and the Sun and Moon are in Capricorn, the *Kumbha-Mela* is at Prayaga.

What Relieves A Headache?

One day a wandering sadhu happened to be sitting at a tea stall opposite a factory which made aspirin. He noticed that many people from the factory came to the tea stall. He quietly listened to their conversations. He heard the tea seller ask one of the factory employees to kindly bring him some aspirin, as he had a terrible headache.

At the same time, he overheard a factory employee saying that he had such a bad headache and needed a hot glass of tea to relieve it.

Observing this interaction, the sadhu thought, "How strange, those who work making aspirin all day come to drink tea to get relief from their headaches, while the tea seller requests aspirin for his headache from the factory employees!" The sadhu wondered, "What really relieves a headache? Aspirin? Tea? Or is it something else?"

Nasrudin and the Red Chilies

O nce Nasrudin traveled to India and visited its capital, Delhi. While wandering through the city, he soon found himself at the marketplace. For some time, he observed the activity there and soon noticed everyone stopping in front of one particular stall, which was selling a beautiful red object which he took to be a fruit. He thought that it must be a delicious fruit since everyone was buying bags full of them. He became so intrigued that he decided to purchase some himself. He was certain that they would taste delicious and bought five pounds of them.

He took the bag and went and sat underneath a nearby tree to enjoy the new fruit. But as he placed one in his mouth and bit into it, he suddenly screamed in pain as it burned his mouth. After sometime, the burning sensation subsided a little, and Nasrudin decided to try another, thinking that perhaps it was an acquired taste. After all, he saw how everyone else purchased so many of them. So he placed another in his mouth and chewed. Then another, and another. Soon his mouth was burning, his eyes started tearing, and his nose ran. But still he did not stop eating them.

Meanwhile a local man noticed Nasrudin and asked why he was eating so many red chilies. Nasrudin explained to the man that this was the first time he had tasted the fruit and was trying to acquire a taste for them. The man said, "My brother, this is not a fruit, it is called a *chilly*, and it is used in small quantities as a spice added to food dishes. They are not meant to be eaten in this manner."

But after listening to the man, Nasrudin once again started eating the chilies. Although his mouth was burning, he continued anyway.

"Why do you continue to eat these chilies," asked the man in surprise, "especially now that you know what they are for?"

"Before I ate them as they were new to me," Nasrudin replied, "but now I eat them because I have paid for them."

This is quite often our own condition. Even though we realize the harmful consequences of certain actions, we continue performing them in the hope that they will become sweet. This is the price of ignorance. We must learn to renounce our attachment to suffering.

Why the Moon Waxes and Wanes

Ages ago, *Chandra*—the Moon married the twenty-seven daughters of Daksha, who are the twenty-seven lunar asterisms called *Nakshatras*. Daksha was one of the powerful sons of Brahma, the Creator. At first Chandra showed equal affection towards all of his wives, but soon he started spending more and more time with the Nakshatra Rohini, his beautiful fourth wife. If one were to look up in the night sky and look towards Rohini, located in the middle of the constellation Taurus, one could see why Chandra favored her over the others.

Nevertheless, since he was spending more time with Rohini, he naturally ignored his other wives. This made Rohini's sisters jealous. Unable to persuade the Moon to spend an equal amount of time with them, they returned to their father's house, angry and dejected. The sisters told their father Daksha why they were so depressed and begged him to do something in order to punish Chandra for making them suffer so much.

After listening to his daughter's complaint against the Moon, Daksha also became angry, and cursed Chandra saying, "O Chandra, I curse you with consumption—the 'wasting disease.' May you gradually lose your luster, so that within fifteen days you will be dead."

Now Daksha was a powerful *Rishi*, and his curse was immediately set in motion. Each day Chandra's natural brilliance became weaker and weaker. His body was ravaged by the disease, and he became paler and thinner with each passing day. No one could cure him, not even the celestial physician.

Rohini, who loved Chandra dearly tried to nurse him back to health, but not even her love could change her father's curse. By the fourteenth day, Chandra's appearance was nothing but a thin sliver in the night sky. Rohini knew that by the next day her beloved husband would be no more.

She could not bare this torture any longer and went to speak with her sisters. She wanted them to come and see how their husband was fading away. She said, "Come my sisters and see your husband, for tomorrow he will surely die."

At first Rohini's sisters started laughing and said that he deserved to suffer for all the sorrow he had caused them. They even began to dance and sing, as if happy at the Moon's death. This caused Rohini great pain, and she burst into tears saying, "Have you no heart? Can you really be happy at the death of your husband, which in turn will make you widows?

Rohini turned in disgust, and returned to her husband's side. But her plea appeared to have an effect on her twenty-six sisters, because one by one they started following her. When they actually saw the condition of their husband, they too became dejected, and with tears in their eyes they prayed for his forgiveness saying, "Oh dear husband, it is because of our jealousy and anger that is causing your death. Please forgive us."

Soon they were all sobbing, and the sky and earth were in darkness. But Rohini suddenly said, "Wait, my sisters. There may still be some hope. Go to our father and falling at his feet, beg him to remove the curse. Now go quickly," Rohini urged them.

The twenty-six sisters immediately left for their father's house. Arriving there, they fell at his feet crying and said, "Oh father, because of your curse our husband Chandra will be dead by tomorrow. Please dear father remove your curse and save his life. We cannot bare to be without his light."

"What!" shouted their father in anger, "First you beg me to punish Chandra and now you are trying to save him. It is your own jealousy which has caused your grief. Don't you know that the words of a *Rishi* cannot be taken back? What I have said must come true."

Hearing Daksha's response, the sisters began to weep even louder and lamented their evil desires. Their remorse appeared to effect their father, and he said in a more gentle and fatherly voice, "Stop your weeping my daughters. Although I can not take back my curse completely, I will modify it for your sake. So listen my children, the disease will ravage your husband's body for fifteen days. He will grow thinner and fainter until the fifteenth day, when he will disappear completely. But the next day, he will start recovering, and day after day he will gain strength and vigor, until the fifteenth day. Then he will once again be his radiant self again. Once again the disease will ravage his body for the next fifteen days making him pale and weak, bringing him close to death. In this way, he will wax and wane each month in unending cycles."

And so it has been ever since that time long ago. We can still see today this monthly cycle of waxing and waning caused by Daksha's curse. From a small sliver, the Moon gradually increases until once again its full orb shines brilliantly in the night sky. But for one day a month, he completely disappears, leaving the world in darkness. Only to reappear the next day, and once again, begin increasing in its radiance, until it becomes completely full.

The Two Drowning Men

O nce two friends were traveling together. One of them was a great devotee of Lord Rama, while the other called on various saviors in times of difficulties. It was the rainy season and the rivers were overflowing their embankments. As they were walking along the banks of the river, suddenly a wave knocked them into the raging waters. The one who was devoted to Rama began calling out continuously, "Rama, Rama, Rama," for help.

But the other man called on one deity after another. At first he called, "Shiva! Shiva! Shiva!" Lord Shiva was about to go and rescue the man when he heard his name being called. But just as he was about to go, the drowning man began calling, "Krishna! Krishna! Krishna! Come and save me!"

Upon hearing this, Shiva said, "Krishna will go and save him" and sat back down to his meditation.

Now when Krishna heard his name being called he too was ready to go and save the man, but just then the man started calling, "Buddha, please save me!" So Krishna stopped and said, "Lord Buddha will go and rescue him."

Buddha, who was deep in meditation, heard his name being called and got up ready to go and save the drowning man. But then suddenly the man started calling, "Jesus! Jesus! Jesus!

Please come and save me!"

Upon hearing this, Lord Buddha decided to let Jesus go and save the man. Unfortunately in the meantime, the poor man drowned.

As long as one has not found a true Master, he or she may go from one teacher to another. After they have found one, there is no further need to go here and there. One may go and meet someone out of respect, but they should understand that their own master is capable of protecting him and taking him to the final goal. Anyone of the above great beings could have saved the drowning man, but it was his lack of one-pointedness which caused his end.

This Too Will Pass!

There was once a great saint who was in the habit of always saying, "Don't worry, this too will pass!" No matter what his devotees said to him about their circumstances, whether positive or negative, this was always his answer. If someone said to him, "O Baba, my wife has run off with another man," or "I have a terrible disease, no money and my children all hate me," he would respond, "Don't worry, this too will pass!" If another person said, "O Baba, I won ten million dollars in the lottery and am now very happy. I have a huge house and a large family that loves me." the saint would simply reply, "Don't worry this too will pass!"

As my Baba would say, the conditions of life are always changing. Like a wheel, with the pairs of opposites as its spokes, rotates continuously bringing now pleasure and then pain, love and hatred, war and peace, wealth and poverty, health and disease. After the one, the other is bound to arise. If sorrow arises, happiness is sure to follow.

The Son of a Donkey

Once Swami Rama Tirtha, referring to a well known sannyasi of his time, who was critical of idol worship, said, "He is the son of a donkey." As a result, the sannyasi filed a libel suit against Swami Rama. Devotees advised him to hire a lawyer but Rama simply said, "I don't require a lawyer. I will fight the case using my own intelligence."

When the case was finally heard, the judge asked Swami Rama, "Did you call the plaintiff 'the son of a donkey?'"

"Yes," Rama replied.

"Well then," asked the judge, "what is your defense to the charges against you?"

Swami Rama said, "Your honor, this person has himself written that one who worships an idol is a donkey. Now his father used to worship an idol, so, according to his own description, his own father was a donkey. As he is his father's son, doesn't it follow that he is the son of a donkey?" Rama asked. Hearing the Swami's reply, the judge immediately dismissed the case.

My Guru used to say that one who has seen God within his own heart will be able to see Him everywhere, even in a stone-idol. But if a person has not found God within, he will never be able to find Him anywhere else. When a person would say that they did not believe in idol worship, Baba would ask, "If God is all pervasive, what makes you think that he is not in the idol as well?"

The Apple and the Two Disciples

There was once a Guru who had many disciples. When the time came to choose a successor he called two of his disciples and handing each of them an apple said, "Go and eat this apple in a spot where nobody is watching you. If you can accomplish this, I will bestow a great title on you. I will also make you my successor, which in turn will give you many disciples."

The two disciples went in opposite directions in search of a spot where they thought no one would see them eat the apple. After going from one place to another, one of them arrived in a deserted forest. After looking around to make sure no one was watching, he quickly ate the apple hoping to be the first to return to his Guru. He in fact had a great desire for his Guru's seat, perhaps even more so than the Guru's knowledge. The disciple rushed back to his Guru's ashram and said, "Guruji, since I ate the apple where nobody was watching and returned first, I should be your successor."

The Guru simply remained silent. After a long time, the other disciple also returned, but he still had the apple in his hand, uneaten. As he placed the fruit before his Master, he said, "Gurudev, I contemplated this question very deeply, and went to many isolated places, yet I could not find a single spot where nobody would see me. Remembering your teachings, wherever I went I found myself surrounded by the five elements of earth, water, fire, air, and space. Even if these were not present, then my own consciousness was present. Therefore, I could not find a single spot where consciousness was not present in some form or another. So I have returned without eating the apple."

The Guru was extremely pleased and embraced the disciple saying, "You indeed deserve to be my successor." And so, the Guru happily installed him on his seat. As for the other disciple, well, he received only an apple.

The Guru frequently tests his disciples, and sometimes these tests may appear very strange. Nevertheless, the disciple must pass them by gaining a proper understanding of his Guru's words, and their exact meaning.

Show Yourself To Anyone But Me

It is the custom in many Muslim countries that a woman should wear a veil so that no one should see her face, except for her husband and immediate family. It is often the case that a husband does not even see his wife's face until the night of their wedding. It is also then that the wife asks the husband who else she could show her face to.

Now this was the case with Nasrudin. He never saw his wife's face until the night of their wedding. When his wife raised her veil for the first time, Nasrudin was shocked, for his new wife was extremely ugly. But it was now too late. He was already married, and had to live with her. However, when his wife asked who else she could show her face to Nasrudin replied, "To anyone else but me."

My Guru would sometimes jokingly tell this story after having just presided over a large wedding ceremony, where often dozens of couples were married at once. He would start laughing so much that he could hardly get to the punch line.

What Even Dogs Don't Eat

O nce during Swami Muktananda's spiritual search, he visited the great Maharashtrian saint, Zipruanna. The saint, who always remained naked was sitting on top of a garbage heap.

Zipruanna, like many great beings often acted in strange ways. In India, whenever one goes to visit a saint, it is customary to bring some fruits, sweets, or some other gift. But whatever Zipruanna received, he used to often throw it to the many dogs and pigs which had gathered around him.

On that day, the saint grabbed Muktananda's money bag and threw all the money to the animals. It so happened that the pouch contained a great deal of money, and Swamiji asked, "What makes you think that dogs and pigs eat money?"

"Then is it proper for a man to eat what even dogs don't eat?" Zipruanna retorted.

Swamiji then asked the saint, "But why must you sit on such rubbish?"

"Muktananda," Zipruanna replied, "inner impurities are far more revolting than this. Don't you know that the human body is a chest full of waste matter?"

Don't Add My Name

Once the saint Abu-ben-Adam was meditating in his room. As he meditated, he suddenly saw a divine light. Out of the light emerged a beautiful maiden who held a book covered with gold. Adam opened his eyes and was still able to see the vision. The maiden showed him the book and he asked what it was.

"In this book," said the maiden, "I write the names of those people who are very brave, who have a lot of faith in their religion, and who pray to God a lot. The names of all those who have become famous are in here, and I wish to add your name as well."

"Please don't add my name," said Abu-ben-Adam, "since I have none of those qualities. I simply try to love my neighbors and remember God." Suddenly the maiden disappeared.

The next day, as Adam was meditating, the light appeared once again. The maiden also appeared, and she was holding the same book. This time she opened it, and inside was written only one name, that of Abu-ben-Adam.

Allah Is Wise!

One day Mullah Nasrudin was lying underneath the shade of a large walnut tree. It was a hot day and he began contemplating the wonders of God's creation. Everything was so perfect he thought.

But as he laid back against the tree, he noticed how large it was, yet it produced such a small fruit. Whereas a nearby pumpkin vine appeared so delicate, and yet it produced such a large fruit.

"Allah is great and Allah is good," said Nasrudin to himself, "but was it really wise of Him to make such a large tree as this to bear such a small fruit, while the pumpkin vine is made to produce such large pumpkins? A vine that cannot even bear the weight of its own fruit? Should walnuts not grow on such spindle vines, and pumpkins on such strong trees?" the Mullah wondered.

As he pondered this idea, Nasrudin dosed off. Only to be awakened by a walnut that fell from the tree, hitting him on the forehead.

"Allah be praised!" shouted Nasrudin, "For if the fruit of this tree were the size of those pumpkins, I would surely be dead. Allah is great! Allah is wise!"

Akbar and the Four Heads

O nce the Moghul Emperor Akbar was riding through the suburbs of Agra accompanied by Birbal and other courtiers. Along the way, they saw a beggar standing by the side of the road, who saluted the king by removing his hat and making a *salaam* to the king. The king in return hailed him with a *salaam-alekam* and removed his crown while he bowed his head.

Now the king's courtiers did not like what Akbar had done and began telling him so. "Your Majesty," one of them said, "it is not right that you should remove the crown from your head and bow to this beggar." Akbar simply said, "We will discuss this tomorrow."

The next day, while everyone was present, including those who had objected to the king's gesture on the previous day, Akbar had ordered the butcher to bring four heads to the great hall. As per the king's instructions the butcher had brought the head of a goat, a ram, a cow and that of a man. When they arrived, the king told the butcher to take the heads to the market and sell them.

The butcher did as he was told and sold the heads of the animals right away, but no one wanted the human head. Unable to sell it, he returned to the palace, and placed the head before the king, saying, "Your Majesty, I was able to immediately sell the heads of the animals, but no one wanted to purchase this human's head."

Turning to those who had criticized his action on the previous day, the king simply said, "See what value a man's head has."

The Kind Hearted Seeker

There was once a Guru who always instructed his disciples not to reveal the secret *mantra* he had initiated them with. One day, a kind hearted seeker went to him and asked to be initiated. The Guru agreed and told him to return early the next morning after taking a bath

The next morning the seeker approached the Guru, and after being initiated by him, the Guru said, "This is a very powerful *mantra*, and you should not divulge it to anyone."

But after his initiation, the young seeker started giving the mantra to many people. When his Guru heard of this, he called his new disciple and started scolding him. "You will go to hell because you divulged the sacred mantra," shouted the Guru.

"And what will happen to those who received the mantra?" inquired the seeker.

"They will of course attain Self-Realization," the Guru replied.

"In that case," said the seeker, "I will be happy to go to hell."

Pleased at the disciples response, the Guru embraced him and said, "You will be my successor."

The disciple in this story is said to have been Sri Ramanuja, the great 11th century Vedantic teacher.

The Dwarf Brahmin

L ong ago, there lived a great monarch named Bali. He was the king of the demons. But having won the grace of God, he dethroned Indra—the king of the gods—and took possession of his kingdom, thereby becoming the monarch of the three worlds.

Now Aditi, the mother of Indra was grieving her son's defeat when her husband, sage Kashyapa, returned home after a long absence. Upon hearing of her unhappiness, the sage tried to comfort her by reminding her that all beings were deluded by the inscrutable power of Maya. "If you wish to experience real happiness," he told her, "then know your inner Self and be free. Worship God who is love and the innermost Self of all beings. Through His grace, you will be free from delusion."

Aditi said, "Then teach me, O sage, how I should worship that great Teacher of all teachers, the Lord of the universe, so that he may fulfill my heart's desire and grant me a boon."

Sage Kashyapa agreed to teach her and told her that God is to be worshipped with one pointed devotion and should be meditated on with a focused mind. She was told to associate with holy persons and try to please them by selfless service.

Having been taught by her husband, Aditi devoted herself completely to her practices. She brought all her passions under control and focused her mind on the inner Lord. In due time, she had a vision of the all pervading Lord, right within her own heart. She became completely absorbed in the vision and her heart melted with divine love. The Lord soon spoke to her saying, "O mother of the gods, I know what you desire. You wish the victory of your son over Bali, the king of the Asuras. But Bali is now under the protection of My power. I am, however, pleased with your devotion and so your desire shall be fulfilled. But how or when this will occur I will not reveal now. However, My power will take birth within your womb as your son."

In time, a son was born to Aditi and Kashyapa. His body had all the auspicious marks of a divine person. However, he was a dwarf, and therefore he became known as the dwarf *brahmin*.

Now Bali, who was still the lord of the three worlds held a great sacrifice and invited all brahmins to attend. In fact, Bali was very generous to all the brahmins.

The dwarf brahmin also decided to attend and set out for the monarch's capital. As he approached the place where the great sacrifice was being held, all the brahmins, as well as Bali himself, noticed a radiance which appeared to illuminate the whole area. As the dwarf brahmin came closer, everyone realized that this radiance was coming from him. Immediately everyone stood up in silent respect for the brahmin, and Bali fell at his feet and addressed the dwarf saying, "Prostrations to you O Brahmin. You must be the embodiment of all the divine powers. By your very presence I feel blessed, as indeed are also my ancestors. Please tell me your wish so that I may please and serve you."

The dwarf replied, "I am very pleased with your reverence and devotion. It is indeed befitting, as you are the grandson of Prahlada, the greatest of the devotees who have blessed this world by their presence. Since you have promised to grant me whatever I ask for, as my needs are little, I ask for only three footsteps of earth."

Hearing the dwarf's request, Bali laughed at such a small wish and said, "Why ask for only three small footsteps of earth, when I can give you a large mansion, and even a large island. Please ask for a greater boon."

The dwarf smiled, and then replied, "I will be satisfied with as much space as can be covered with three steps, I seek no more."

Although still amused by this meager request from the dwarf, Bali promised to grant his desire and asked him to accept the boon. But at that moment, Sukracharya, Bali's Guru and priest, intervened saying, "By granting this gift, you will bring a great catastrophe to yourself. Do you not recognize that this son of Sage Kashyapa and Aditi is the very embodiment of the Divine. With his form alone, he can cover the whole universe. With his three steps, he will cover the three worlds and will then return them to Indra. One step of this dwarf will cover the earth, the second step will reach heaven, and with the third step there will be no place left."

Bali now realized the magnitude of his promise, but he was nevertheless not unhappy having made it. He felt that no matter what, he should keep his word. After all, he thought to himself, "I have been born into the family of Prahlada." Therefore, turning to the dwarf, and with folded hands, he said with reverence, "Please accept the gift."

Then suddenly, as he looked at the dwarf, he saw the whole universe existing in him. As the dwarf took his first step, he covered the whole earth, his body covered the sky, and his arms embraced the four directions. With his second step, he covered the heavens and the rest of the universe. As there was no other place for his third step, he asked Bali, "Now where shall I place my third step."

Bali humbly and reverently said, "Although it is true that there is no place for your third stride, I must keep my word. Therefore, I humbly offer my own head, so please place your foot on my head. For I now and forever belong to you. I, who have been blinded for so long by my pride of power and wealth have been purified by your sight."

The Lord of the universe, in the form of a dwarf said, "You indeed are my devotee and are true to your word. Your gift to me will be remembered in ages to come and glorified in both heaven and earth."

The Man and His Shadow

There was once a man who was afraid of both his shadow and his footprints. Whenever he saw them, he would try to run away from them, but wherever he went, there too were his shadow and footprints. It did not matter whether he ran forward or backwards, or from side to side, they appeared to chase him everywhere.

Anxiety over his shadow and footprints so consumed the man that one day he decided to try and outrun them. But looking back he noticed that they were still following him, and so he ran faster. But no matter how fast he ran, his shadow and footprints were right behind him.

At last, the poor unfortunate man simply collapsed from exhaustion and died on the spot. As he fell forward, his shadow disappeared and the footprints also came to an end.

The storyteller remarks that, "If that poor man had simply sat underneath a shady tree, both his shadow and footprints would have disappeared." My own Guru would also say that instead of running around frantically all the time, if we would sit calmly in meditation for sometime, we would experience great inner peace. Therefore, we should try to develop a genuine interest in meditation.

The Argument Over
The Unborn Child

O nce a landlord heard a loud argument coming from his upstairs tenants. They were a young couple and had lived happily there for a number of years without incident.

The argument was becoming more heated and the landlord was afraid that some violence would occur. He decided to go upstairs and see if he could help relieve some of the tension.

He went up and knocked on their door and inquired if he could be of some help. The couple invited him in and proceeded to explain the reason for their argument.

"I feel our son should become a lawyer," said the husband, "but my wife wants him to become a doctor."

"A doctor is more sensitive and makes plenty of money," interjected the wife, "and at the same time he brings relief to others. Lawyers, on the other hand, tend to lack compassion."

"What foolishness," yelled the husband. "Lawyers make a lot more money, and when he becomes successful and gets big cases he will also gain position and prestige." Suddenly the argument broke out once again.

"Calm yourselves," said the landlord. "This should not be too difficult to solve. But first, please bring your son so that I may question him about his interests."

"What son?" asked the couple.

"The son you have been arguing about," answered the neighbor.

"But we have no son yet," said the couple. "We have not even conceived a child yet!"

The poor landlord raised his hands up in resignation and said, "You have been arguing so much over a child who is not even born yet, and may possibly never become born?"

The child is not even born and the parents are already planning and arguing over the child's profession. This is exactly what happens in our minds, which is constantly engaged in planning for tomorrow and even years into the future. The mind becomes agitated worrying about even that which has not even occurred. Be calm and experience the silent moment.

Guilty!

Not long ago a newspaper reported on an accident which occurred during an attempted robbery. A thief had broken into a rich business man's home. However he was interrupted by the early return of the homeowner and tried to make his escape out through the third floor balcony. As luck would have it, the balcony collapsed and the thief was killed.

Now one would think that would have been the end of the story. But actually it was only the beginning. The thief's relatives decided to bring a lawsuit against the homeowner charging that their relative's death was due to the defective balcony, therefore the business man should be held responsible. The case went before the courts. When the judge asked the homeowner what his defense was to the charges, the business man said that he should not be held responsible since the house was over fifty years old. "And besides," the man added, "I did not build the house or the balcony. But I know who the builder is, and it is he who should be held responsible, not me."

The judge thought that the man had a point and so he summoned the old builder to his court. The judge asked the man if he had built the balcony, and the man said he had. "Well," said the judge, "what is your defense for building such a poor structure? Do you know that a man has been killed while standing on it?"

The old builder thought for a moment, and then said that he should not be held responsible for that. "It is true, Your Honor, that the balcony was defective," the man said, "but I remember being distracted that day by a beautiful prostitute who kept walking up and down the street right in front of where I was working. My mind was so distracted that I could not focus on my work. Therefore, she should be held responsible for such a catastrophe, not me." He also added that he knew where the prostitute was living.

The judge thought it was a reasonable defense. After all, he thought, who can keep their attention on their work when a beautiful woman is marching up and down in front of a person?

The prostitute who was now in her nineties was brought before the judge. The judge asked, "Did you parade back and forth in front of this poor man years ago while he was trying to build the balcony of a certain house?" The old woman thought for a moment and said she had.

"So," the judge exclaimed, "you are responsible for the death of a young man."

"But Your Honor," the old woman said, "I remember that day very well. You see," the old prostitute continued, "I remember why I had to walk up and down that street so many times that day. There was an old jeweler to whom I had given some items to, and he had me return over a half dozen times, but each time he had not finished the work. And so it was for that reason that I had to walk in front of this builder so many times that day. Therefore, I should not be held responsible for this crime since it was the jeweler's fault and not mine."

The judge agreed and called the old jeweler to court. The jeweler was now practically on his death bed, but when the judge told him that he was responsible for the death of the thief, he too had a story to tell. He said that the reason why he had to ask the prostitute to return to his shop so many times was because a wealthy business man had unexpectedly ordered some special ornaments, and demanded that they be ready that day. And that was why he could not finish the prostitute's work on time and therefore had to ask her to return a number of times.

"And who was that wealthy man?" asked the judge. When the jeweler described the man and where he lived, it turned out to be the house where the accident had occurred. In fact, it was the father of the business man who was originally charged. However, the man said that since it was his father who had given the jeweler the special order, and he was now dead he was not responsible. But the judge reasoned that since it was his father who was the cause of all this, and his son had inherited everything from his father, he also inherited his crime. Therefore, "Guilty," shouted the judge.

The Flower Is White!

The great Maharashtrian saint, Samartha Ramdass, was said to be such a great devotee of Sri Rama that whenever he recited the Ramayana, Hanuman would appear in disguise among the audience.

On one such occasion, Ramdass was describing the garden in which Sita was held captive in Ravana's kingdom. As if in a mystical trance, Ramdass described the various trees, shrubs, and a particular type of flower, the oleander, which he said was white.

Upon hearing this last statement, Hanuman jumped up and said, "The flower was red."

"They were white," Ramdass said firmly.

Hanuman revealed himself and said, "I should know since I was there, and you were not, the flowers were red."

Unable to come to an agreement they decided to call on Sita to resolve the matter. When Sita appeared, Hanuman said, "This foolish person insists that those flowers in Ravana's garden were white, even though I have been trying to explain to him that they were red. Please correct him and tell him the actual color of the flowers."

"The flowers were of course white," Sita answered with a smile.

"How can you say that," asked Hanuman in astonishment, "I was there and they were red."

"My child," said Sita lovingly, "indeed you were there. But as you were filled with rage against Ravana, your eyes saw everything red. On the other hand, Ramdass is seeing everything through his clear mystical eye, and he sees things as they are."

Indeed, we can not always trust even our own senses. For they are often colored by the six enemies: anger, lust, desire, delusion, greed and pride. Only when the mind is calm do we see clearly.

The Guru's Teaching

There was a great saint named Kabir. He had a disciple who lived with him named Kamal. He would later become a great saint himself due to his selfless service and complete surrender to his Guru.

But once, someone insulted Kabir in Kamal's presence. Kamal became very angry with the man and got into a fight with him.

Now Kabir heard about the incident and called Kamal. When Kamal arrived, Kabir said, "Kamal, you are of no use. You are neither a devotee nor a disciple. However, if you wish, you can stay here as a laborer."

Kamal was confused and asked his master what he had done.

"Didn't you fight with that man?" asked Kabir.

"Yes I did," replied Kamal.

"When did I teach you to fight with anyone?" inquired Kabir. "I have never taught you such things. What is the purpose of staying with me when you don't learn what I teach?"

In the same way, followers of different religious groups fight among themselves, Baba would comment. *In fact, we should not involve ourselves in any religious conflicts.*

A Blade of Grass

O nce, many ages ago, Indra and the other gods returned
to their celestial realm after conquering the demons.
The victory inflated Indra's ego and the supreme
Lord wanted to teach him a lesson, that in fact, everything that
happens in the universe is because of His power alone. The Lord
decided to take the form of a *yaksha*, a demigod, and went and
sat in a nearby tree close to Indra's palace.

When he heard of the *yaksha's* presence, Indra sent Agni, the
god of fire to find out who the being was. After being questioned
by Agni about who he was, and why he had come there, the
yaksha simply said, "I am an ordinary *yaksha*, but may I know
who you are?"

"Can't you see that I am the god of fire?" Agni answered,
somewhat annoyed. "With my power I can burn the three
worlds," he continued.

"I see!" said the *yaksha* somewhat doubtful. "If you can burn
the three worlds," he challenged, "then let me see you burn this
blade of grass!"

So he threw a blade of grass on the ground and Agni tried to
burn it. But no matter how intense his heat got, he could not
burn it. He was amazed and returned to Indra. He then narrated
to the leader of the gods what had occurred.

Puzzled at this, Indra decided to send Vayu, the god of wind to question the stranger. Upon reaching the spot, Vayu boasted that he could toss the very tree that the *yaksha* was sitting on into the sky.

The *yaksha* smiled saying, "If that is so, then first move a blade of grass," and he tossed one to the ground.

Vayu tried, but even after becoming a powerful gale force, the small blade of grass was not moved. Overcome, Vayu immediately returned to Indra, telling him what had happened.

Although Indra was now fearful about this mysterious stranger, he was also curious as to his identity. He therefore decided to go and see the *yaksha* himself. However, by the time he reached the spot, the *yaksha* had disappeared, and in his place was the Lord's divine power, the Mother of the Universe. The universal mother explained to Indra that the *yaksha* was none other than the Lord himself and said, "It is only by His power that fire burns, the wind blows, the sun shines, and everything that exists, exists. Not even a blade of grass moves without His will."

The Need for a Guru

In the month of October in the year 1270 C.E., a boy was born in the Indian state of Maharashtra. His name was Namdev, and he was destined to become one of the greatest saints of India. When he was born, an astrologer predicted he would write countless poems (*abhangas*).

Even as a child his intense devotional nature was obvious. A story is told how once when his father, who was a tailor, had to go out of town on business, he instructed Namdev, who was only a child of about six to perform the daily family worship. Namdev was overjoyed since he had always sat with his father during the ceremony watching very closely everything he did.

Now as part of the worship, his father would offer milk to the image of Vitthal (God), and so Namdev did the same. But when he noticed that the milk was left untouched, Namdev felt extremely hurt. He had always thought that the idol actually drank the milk offered by his father. But now, for some reason, God would not accept his offering.

This made Namdev feel very sad. "Why will you not accept my offering?" Namdev asked the image. "Do you not love me?"

When he did not receive a response, he became so overwhelmed with emotion that he began to cry uncontrollably. His mother tried to pacify him but Namdev would not listen. He vowed that he would remain sitting there until the Lord accepted his offering.

And there he sat, for what seemed to be the longest time, praying that God would drink the milk. His mother tried to explain to him that God did not really drink the milk, but Namdev could not be persuaded. He was determined to convince God to accept the milk from him, as he had always done for his father.

A long time passed and still nothing happened. But then suddenly, with his mother sitting by his side, the milk began to disappear from the cup. It was as if an invisible being had started sucking up the milk with a straw. Soon the cup was empty. Namdev became ecstatic and began to dance around the image. His mother too, shaken by the experience started crying with joy.

As Namdev grew older, he started visiting the sacred town of Pandharpur. Since Pandharpur was the sacred hub for all the saints of Maharashtra, Namdev soon decided to settle there. However, although Namdev had been on the spiritual path from an early age, still he did not have a Guru. A spiritual master is considered extremely important if one wishes to make any advances in the spiritual life. So one day there was a gathering of saints in Pandharpur. This group was headed by the young yogi and saint, Jnaneshwar. In fact, Namdev was only a few years older than Jnaneshwar. The group included Jnaneshwar's brothers and sister, Gora the Potter, Samvata the Gardener, Narahari the Goldsmith, and Chokha the Untouchable.

Namdev decided to join the group and sat with them and

performed *kirtana*, which is the singing of devotional hymns and poems.

After the kirtana was over, everyone continued to sit together, because sometimes a religious discussion would arise. But that day, Jnaneshwar told Gora to go around the room and see whether everyone there was spiritually mature or not. As Gora was a potter, he walked around the room and started tapping each and everyone of them as he would a pot. Potters can determine if a pot is 'baked' or 'unbaked' simply by the sound it makes. Now, when he tapped Namdev with his stick, Namdev yelled out, "Hey, what do you think you're doing?" Gora immediately pronounced Namdev to be 'unbaked.'

Now, since Namdev was the only one considered by Gora to be 'unbaked', he became unhappy and discouraged. After all, he had a number of powerful spiritual experiences and thought himself to be close to God. But in fact, even with all his experiences, Namdev had still only a narrow view of God.

In any case, Jnaneshwar took pity on him and explained to him that the reason why he had not yet attained spiritual maturity was because he did not have a Guru. "Go and see Visoba Khechara," the young yogi told him, "he will bless you."

Although Visoba Khechara was older than Jnaneshwar, he himself was the disciple of Jnaneshwar's younger brother Sopana, who in turn had been initiated by Jnaneshwar himself.

Namdev immediately set out in search of Visoba Khechara, who he was told stayed in a certain Shiva temple. When Namdev reached the spot, he went inside the Nagnatha temple where he saw what appeared to be an old man suffering from leprosy lying on the floor with his feet resting on the sacred *Shiva-linga*.

Namdev was shocked at this sacrilege and sternly reprimanded the old man telling him to remove his feet at once. The old man, who was none other than Visoba Khechara, told him that he was too weak to move them himself, and asked Namdev to place them where God was not present.

This remark apparently had a powerful effect on Namdev's mind, and it made him instantly realize that God was omnipresent. Namdev immediately dropped to his knees and bowed at Visoba's feet asking him to initiate him into the spiritual path.

Visoba studied him for a moment, and then placed his hand on Namdev's head in blessing. From that moment onwards, Namdev's spiritual life began to blossom. His spiritual unfoldment is revealed in the thousands of *abhangas* he wrote. Regarding the blessing he received from Visoba, Namdev wrote:

> *"The secret has been revealed to me. The hand of protection has been placed on my head. Nama (Namdev) has been made bodiless. Visoba Khechar, who is ever intoxicated with the love of the Lord, has initiated me. Khechar told me that Guru is knowledge. He has taken Nama to imperishable regions."*

Namdev also became very close to Jnaneshwar, and when the young yogi wanted to go on a pilgrimage to northern India, Namdev accompanied him. But shortly after the conclusion of the pilgrimage, Jnaneshwar, at the young age of twenty-one departed from this world. This effected Namdev very deeply, and he decided to leave Pandharpur on another pilgrimage. This would take him throughout northern India and would last for many years. Eventually he would settle in the small village of Ghuman in the Punjab, where he spent the last eighteen years of his life. He would live for over fifty years after Jnaneshwar's death.

Some say that he died in that village and is also buried there, but others say that he returned to Pandharpur just before his death and died there in the year 1350. He is actually buried underneath the front door of the temple opposite the tomb of Chokamela.

In any case, Namdev has not only inspired the saints of Maharashtra, like Tukaram and Eknath, but also many of those in northern India. His poems and hymns have been sung by Kabir and his followers, as well as Nanak and others in the Sikh tradition. One can find sixty-one of his poems in the Guru Granth, the holy scripture of the Sikhs.

This story of how Namdev found his Guru is told to illustrate that even if one has divine visions and is apparently close to God, he still requires a Guru to destroy the trappings of the ego. Only the Guru is capable of such a task.

Speak the Truth...
Never Become Angry!

D ronacharya was the teacher of the princely Pandavas and their cousins the Kauravas. On the day he began teaching them, the first lesson was, "Always speak the truth, never become angry." When saying this, he told the princes that they should be prepared to repeat this lesson the next day.

"Since there are only a few words," the boys said to themselves, "this will be easy to memorize."

The next day when they came to school, the teacher asked them one at a time to stand up, and repeat the previous day's lesson. Each boy got up and repeated, "Always speak the truth, never become angry."

However, when it was the turn of the virtuous Yudhishthira, he could only say, "Speak the truth..." and said that he had not yet been able to learn the second part of the lesson.

"Just keep repeating it over and over again," the teacher told him, "and I'm sure you'll know it by tomorrow."

The next day all the other students again repeated the lesson, but once again Yudhishthira could only repeat the first part, "Speak the truth..."

"And what about the second part?" asked the teacher.

"I still haven't learnt that part yet," answered Yudhishthira.

This went on for a number of days, but still Yudhishthira had not learnt his lesson. Dronacharya was disappointed and sternly talked to the boy saying, "A whole week has passed and still you haven't been able to learn such a simple lesson."

Dronacharya thought that he could beat some sense into the boy and started beating him with a stick. But Yudhishthira just stood there calmly taking each stroke.

Dronacharya was surprised at how well the boy was taking this. He knew that if he had beaten any of the other princes like Duryodhana or Bheema, they would have probably struck him back. But here was Yudhishthira, the future Emperor of India, taking it silently and even cheerfully.

The teacher asked the boy why he was having such a difficult time learning such a simple lesson. "You say it is simple and that a whole week has passed," answered Yudhishthira, "but even if years were to pass, I'm not sure that I could learn this lesson fully."

"What do you mean?" asked Dronacharya in surprise.

"My idea of a lesson," answered Yudhishthira, "is not simply to repeat it by saying 'never become angry'. To me, learning this lesson means 'never to become angry', and unless I have achieved that, I can't say that I have learnt the lesson properly. But now that you have given me this beating, I can say that I have *almost* learnt the second part of the lesson. But I still felt a little anger when you were beating me."

This story from the Mahabharata teaches us that we should not learn things simply by rote. Like Yudhishthira, we should be able to absorb the spirit of the lesson and be able to put into practice the rules of good conduct. The other boys simply memorized "never become angry," but never actually practiced not becoming angry.

The Dark Age

Towards the end of the last age, the sages had gathered in the forest of Naimisharanya in northern India. Soon Brahma the Creator arrived and a discussion ensued about the effects of the coming age of Kali Yuga, known as the dark age. "What will be its effects and how will sincere seekers free themselves from its influence?" they asked one another,

While they were engaged in this discussion, suddenly a naked demonic figure appeared dancing wildly in front of the assembled company. In one hand, he held a long drooling tongue and in the other, his sex organ.

"Who are you?" asked the outraged sages, "and why have you come to this holy spot in such an offensive condition?"

"I am the spirit of Kali Yuga," said the creature, "and in the coming age my power will overtake the whole world. By speaking lies, deceit, and slander through the tongue, and by the perversions of the sex organ, I will corrupt and control the entire world. Even great sages will fall by my power."

The assembled sages were horrified to hear about the coming age. But Brahma made Kali promise not to effect those sincere seekers who were performing spiritual practices (*sadhana*), as well as those who chanted the name of God. Because it is so difficult to remain undisturbed in the Kali Yuga, a great deal of emphasis has been placed on chanting God's name. In fact, spiritual realization which is so difficult to obtain in the other ages, is said to become easy in the Kali Yuga, simply by chanting God's name.

This story is recounted in the Guru-charitra, a book written in the Marathi language which contains a number of stories, as well as a version of the Guru Gita. Besides informing us that the dark age is perverted due to the inability of controlling our sexual passions and one's tongue or the organ of speech, we are shown a simple method for achieving self-realization by using the tongue to chant God's holy name.

Nasrudin and Family Lineage

O nce, Mullah Nasrudin was giving a religious lecture to some young students. He was telling them that God had created the whole Universe with all its various inhabitants including all of humanity.

Upon hearing this, one of the students raised his hand and said to the Mullah, "Oh Nasrudin, you are mistaken. Modern science has taught us that we have evolved from the jungle apes not from God."

"At the moment I am not speaking about your own family lineage," answered the Mullah calmly, "but of the human family in general."

Vishnu and Lakshmi

Once Narada, the wandering minstrel arrived in the heavenly region of Lord Vishnu. The Lord was lying on Ananta, the primordial serpent, while Goddess Lakshmi was massaging his legs. But on this occasion, the Lord appeared to be in a somber mood, as if something was troubling Him. When Narada noticed this, he asked, "Lord, why do you look so troubled?"

"Aah Narada," the Lord sighed, "Lakshmi is my problem."

"What do you mean?" Narada asked in bewilderment.

"I'll show you what I mean," the Lord answered.

Suddenly, the Lord of the Universe took on the form of a Scholar and went to a small town on earth. There he began giving daily spiritual talks which were delivered with such beauty and devotion that soon the entire town's population stopped everything they were doing and began attending his discourses. Everyone became entranced listening to the Scholar's wisdom. And soon, they began developing devotion for God which in turn brought joy and harmony to the whole town. This now seemed to be transformed into heaven itself.

Now as the old saying goes, 'Where Vishnu is, his consort Lakshmi, the goddess of prosperity is sure to follow.' She soon arrived disguised as a withered old woman, and just as the daily discourse was about to start, she went to a nearby house and asked for some water.

As the woman of the house was anxious not to miss the start of the day's discourse, she quickly handed the old woman a cup of water. But as soon as the metal cup touched Lakshmi's hand, it turned into gold.

"What has happened to my cup?" the lady of the house said in astonishment, "It's turned into solid gold!"

"Yes," answered Lakshmi with a smile, "it is so." "You see," she explained, "my hand has this effect. Everything it touches turns into gold. But you may keep the cup."

Within a short time the news of the cup being turned into gold had spread throughout the small town. And, instead of attending the Scholar's discourse, many of the women decided to wait at home hoping that the old woman would visit their house.

And so she did. In their greed, the women would hand Lakshmi all types of kitchen utensils for her to touch. Soon all of their plates, mugs, cooking pots, and other utensils were turned into gold. Even the men found ways to profit from this unexpected good-fortune and soon not one person attended the Scholar's discourses.

Now, the saints say that the Lord stays only where there is true devotion and love, and since no one now went to Him, Vishnu immediately left that place. And of course, where Vishnu goes, Lakshmi follows. As they left, devotion for God quickly declined and their prosperity also diminished. And soon the townspeople returned to their old life style.

Indeed, devotion for God brings blessings and prosperity. However, the moment one starts to chase after Lakshmi and forgets Vishnu, the Lord departs, and of course, Lakshmi will soon follow.

Bharata
India's Ancient Monarch

L ong ago the royal sage Rishabha had a son named Bharata. Bharata became such a great monarch that the country which today we know as India became known as *Bharata-varsha*, or the land of Bharata. Before that, the country was known as Ajanabha.

This great king ruled his subjects with such devotion that he was loved by all. This attitude of Bharata also purified his heart. Every act he performed was for the benefit of all. He never thought of personal gain.

Now in his old age, he desired to retire to the forest for spiritual practices. The king therefore divided his kingdom among his five sons. He retired to a forest in the Himalayas and built a small cottage on the banks of the river Gandaki.

In that isolated forest, he performed his daily worship day after day with diligence. In this way, months passed and then years.

One day a doe came to drink near the place where the sage meditated. At the same time, a tiger was heard roaring nearby. This terrified the doe and without pausing, she jumped trying to furiously cross the river. Being with child, the sudden exertion and fright made her give birth right then and there.

Unfortunately the exertion also killed her, and the new fawn fell into the fast moving river currents and was being swept away. Seeing the tragic condition of the fawn, Bharata immediately jumped into the river and rescued the newborn deer. He took the small creature to his cottage and dried it off. He started caring for him as a mother would her own child.

In time, the helpless creature grew into a beautiful deer. Bharata became more and more fond of the deer and so attached to it, that whenever the deer did not return in time from his normal grazing, he would worry that some tiger had attacked it. Otherwise, he could not imagine why the deer was so late in returning.

Some years passed in this way, then one day, knowing that his death was near, the sage laid himself down to die. But instead of focusing his attention on the inner divinity, his mind started thinking about the deer lying besides him. While gazing at the deer's face, Bharata breathed his last.

Because of this, in his next birth Bharata was reborn as a deer. However, no spiritual effort goes to waste. The new born deer called Jatismara remembered his past birth. Being in an animal's body, he could not speak, but even so, he enjoyed grazing alone near ashrams of great saints.

After living the normal number of years, the deer died and was reborn as the youngest son of a wealthy Brahmin. In that life, he also remembered his previous births, but this time he became determined from an early age not to entangle himself in worldly life again. As he grew older, although he was physically strong and healthy, he did not speak. Fearing of becoming entangled again in worldly life, he lived like a dumb-witted boy. He was always thinking about his inner Self. In fact, he lived simply to exhaust his remaining *karmas*.

When Bharata's father finally died thinking him to be a fool, his brothers decided to divide the property amongst themselves. They gave him only barely enough food to live on. Their wives also treated him harshly and practically turned him into a slave. They forced all of their heavy chores on him, and would abuse him with harsh words.

Bharata remained silent throughout all the abuse and simply did as they wished. When they all would gang up on him, he would go and sit under a nearby tree until they calmed down. Sometimes he would remain absolutely still in deep meditation for hours.

Now it so happened that one day, when the brother's wives had been extremely cruel to him, Bharata was sitting under a nearby tree when king Rahugana happened to pass by. He was being carried on his palanquin. One of the bearers suddenly took ill, and the king's men began searching for someone to replace him.

They saw Bharata's robust appearance. They asked him if he would replace the sick bearer. Bharata remained silent. Even though his eyes were partially opened, his gaze was always within. Not receiving an answer, the king's soldiers grabbed him and placed the pole on his shoulder.

Bharata walked along with the others in an ecstatic mood. But after going just a short distance, the king complained that the palanquin was not being carried smoothly enough. Looking out to the bearers, he noticed that it was Bharata who was making the movements uneven. The king angrily called out to him saying, "O fool, if your shoulder is giving you pain, then rest yourself."

Everyone stopped, and Bharata laid his pole on the ground. Suddenly, for the first time in his life, Bharata opened his mouth and spoke saying, "O king, whom do you call a fool? Who are you asking to lay down the palanquin? Who are you saying is weary? Who are you addressing as 'You'? If by the word 'you,' you mean this clod of flesh made up of the same elements as yours, that can not be, for it is unconscious and knows no fatigue or pain. If by 'you' you mean the mind, than that too is the same universal principle. But if you mean something even deeper than these, then it is the Self. This Reality in me is the same as within you. It is indeed the Self of the Universe. Can this Self ever be weary or in pain?" he asked.

"O king," Bharata continued, "along the path I noticed many small creatures crawling about. Not wishing to harm them, I would move to one side or the other. Because of this, the palanquin was carried unevenly. But the Self was never weak or tired. Being omnipotent and omnipresent, it never even carried the pole of the palanquin."

Hearing the sage's remarks, the king jumped from the palanquin and bowed at Bharata's feet begging his pardon. The king had a deep interest in the sacred knowledge and Bharata instructed him for some time. Finally, he told the king, "O king Rahugana, this world will always keep you trapped, therefore give up all, and with the sword of knowledge sharpened by service,

143

devotion, and meditation, cut the bonds of ignorance."

Having received the great teaching, King Rahugana returned to his kingdom, meditated on, and finally realized the Truth he had learnt. Meanwhile, Bharata continued to teach others until the end of his life. Ever since that time, India has been called Bharata. From this story, we can see the value the residents of that great country place on spiritual wisdom.

A Liver For The Lord

There was once a king who had no children. As he was a devotee of Sage Narada, he approached him and asked him to bless him with a child.

Narada considered himself to be a great devotee of Lord Vishnu and said to the king, "Don't worry, this will be an easy task," and he proceeded to instruct the king on how to perform certain rituals for obtaining children.

The king and his queen followed the procedure, but after a number of years they still had no children. He again approached Narada, who was now also feeling a bit apprehensive and dismayed at the poor results. Narada decided to approach Vishnu and said, "Lord, this man and his wife are very great devotees of mine. Please bless them with a child."

The Lord said, "Let us look at their *karmic* records and see if they deserve a child. If so, we'll certainly give them one."

But when the king and queen's records were examined, it was found that the king did not deserve a child. "This man is not destined to have a child for at least ten life times," said the Lord, "so you better instruct him to immerse himself in devotion if you wish to help him."

Narada returned to his devotees and told them what the

Lord had said. But at Narada's encouragement, the king now started chanting the divine name in order to purify his negative *karmas*.

Some time elapsed, and one day a great devotee of the Lord happened to pass by the palace and started shouting, "One *chapati*, one child; two *chapatis*, two children; three *chapatis*, three children!"

Hearing this, the queen grabbed three pieces of bread (*chapatis*) and ran to the saint and lovingly placed them in his hand hoping for the best. In due course of time, she gave birth to three children.

Some time after the birth of the third child, Narada happened to visit the king's court. Seeing the children playing in the courtyard Narada asked, "Whose children are these?"

"Ours," smiled the king.

"Impossible," said Narada, "the Lord Himself told me that you could not have children for at least ten life times."

The queen told Narada about the saint and narrated to him what had happened. Angry, and feeling personally insulted, Narada immediately went to Vishnu's abode in order to voice his disappointment and obvious unreliability of the Lord's word.

However, the Lord, who is omniscient knew Narada's thoughts, and when he saw him approaching in the distance, he laid down and pretended to be suffering from a terrible abdominal pain. When Narada arrived, he noticed people running around in a panic and was horrified to see the Lord lying on the bed groaning in pain.

"What has happened?" Narada asked the Lord's physician.

"The Lord is extremely ill," answered the physician sadly, "and the only medicine that can alleviate His pain is made from the liver of a true devotee."

"Oh Narada, you know many devotees, can you get one for me?" asked the Lord.

"I'll get you not only one," said Narada proudly, "but many."

Immediately Narada set off in search of a liver. He started asking all his devotees if they would donate their liver for the Lord. But although many said that they would like to, everyone gave some excuse for not being able to do so. One said that he was still young and was just about to marry. Another said that he had to look after his aged parents. Finally Narada reached the palace and asked the king and queen, but they said, "Well, of course we would be happy to give our liver, but we now have three small children to look after."

In fact, no one was prepared to part with their liver. Dejected, Narada returned to the Lord's house.

"Did you bring a liver?" asked the Lord.

"No," replied Narada sadly, "I was unsuccessful."

Feigning surprise, the Lord said, "There is a devotee of mine sitting on the banks of a river. Go to him and tell him that I am in pain and require a liver."

Narada immediately went to the devotee and found him sitting in deep meditation. As the scriptures say that one should not disturb a person who is in *samadhi*, Narada stood quietly waiting for him to emerge from his deep spiritual state. In fact, this was the same saint who had blessed the king and queen with the three children.

After sometime, the saint finally opened his eyes and saw Narada standing before him. Bowing to the sage, the devotee apologized for keeping him waiting. "Why have you come?," he asked Narada humbly.

"I have come with the terrible news that the Lord is suffering with great pain due to some illness. The physicians say that he can be cured only by the liver of a true devotee. I have asked many people, but as yet I have not been able to get one."

The devotee suddenly became angry and said, "Why have you waited so long and allowed the Lord to continue to suffer. You should have ripped my liver out of my body. In fact, the Lord can have this whole body. Let us go quickly to the Lord so we can alleviate his suffering."

They immediately set off for Vishnu's abode. However, when they arrived, strange to say, Lord Vishnu was sitting quite normally as if nothing had happened.

"Lord, here is someone willing to give his liver for the relief of your ailment," Narada said excitedly.

"It is not necessary," said the Lord, "I am feeling much better now. But tell me, why did you find it necessary to travel throughout the three worlds in search of a liver? Don't you have one? You consider yourself such a great devotee, why didn't you offer your own liver? Look at this great and true devotee of mine. Because he has given his whole life to Me and is even willing to give his body without hesitation, his word and blessing has great power. It can even change the law of destiny."

The Saint and the Foolish Man

Once a supposed sadhu visited the ashram of the great saint, Siddharudha Swami, and asked him for some money to purchase *ganja* (marijuana). Siddharudha became very angry and said, "You call yourself a sadhu. Why are you asking me for money to buy *ganja*?"

Suddenly the sadhu started cursing Siddharudha and used a particularly fowl language that when translated into English means something like "I'm going to sleep with your wife." But of course he used a much more vulgar word than sleep.

Upon hearing this foul language, the saint's disciples who were sitting around him suddenly pounced on the man.

"Stop, Stop!" yelled Siddharudha to his disciples. "What are you doing? Calm yourselves," he said, "there is no need for this. Have you forgotten my teachings of non-violence?"

"This scoundrel swore at you and your wife in such a fowl manner," his agitated disciples replied.

"Have you forgotten that I am a *sannyasi*," Siddharudha asked, "and therefore do not have a wife? This man has therefore insulted someone who does not exist."

The Most Foolish Men of Delhi

Birbal was a wise and quick-witted *brahmin* in the court of Emperor Akbar. The king had met his minister when Birbal was still a young boy. The good natured minister was not only loved by the king but also by the people. He was extremely clever, and his sound advice assisted Akbar on many occasions.

Nevertheless, in jest, Akbar tried many times to trip Birbal up hoping to prove him wrong. Once he thought of a task which he was certain Birbal could not carry out. So one day, the king said, "Birbal, I have met the wisest men in the kingdom. But I would now like to meet the most foolish. Could you possibly find me six of the most foolish men in Delhi?"

Without hesitation Birbal said, "I will try, Your Majesty."

The next morning Birbal set out in search of the city's most foolish men. He walked through the narrow lanes of the old city looking carefully at every one he met. Then suddenly, he saw a man lying on the ground with his two arms outstretched over his head, as if frozen in position. The man appeared to be struggling to get up, but for some reason he could not. Birbal walked over to him and asked what the problem was.

"I slipped and fell in this puddle on my way to buy some fabric for my wife," the man said, "and I can't seem to get up."

"Well why don't you just use your hands to get up?" suggested Birbal.

"Oh no," replied the man, "if I change the position of my hands, I will then loose the exact measurement for the length of cloth my wife wants."

"Aah," said Birbal smiling to himself, "in that case I better help you get up." Birbal immediately grabbed the man's torso and helped him to his feet.

"Oh, thank you very much," the man said gratefully.

"What is your name?" Birbal asked.

"My name is Ali," the man answered.

Birbal knew that he had found his first foolish man and said, "You could be of some help to me Ali. Would you mind coming with me?"

"Not at all," answered Ali, and began following Birbal without even asking why and still holding his arms outstretched.

Now after walking for some distance, Birbal suddenly noticed a man walking backwards through the city streets. As he was curious, he began walking alongside the man, and after sometime he asked him why he was walking backwards.

"Why, to see where I am coming from, of course," answered the man without missing a step.

"But is it not better to see where you are going?" asked Birbal.

"Why anyone can see where they are going," the man answered, "but there are only a few of us who can see where we have been."

When he heard this answer, Birbal immediately knew he had found his second foolish man. He introduced himself and asked the man if he would mind going with him. "Not at all," answered the man, who said his name was Govinda. Being an adventurous soul, he too began following Birbal, of course still walking backwards.

After walking for some time with Ali and Govinda behind him, Birbal noticed a man riding a horse, and at the same time he was carrying a bundle of fire-wood on top of his head. Thinking this was unusual, Birbal approached the man and asked, "Why are you carrying that fire-wood on your head instead of placing it on the horse's back?"

"Oh no," the man said with alarm, "I can't do that. This poor horse is old and weak. Besides having to carry me, if I were to add this extra load, it might kill him."

Hearing the man's reply, Birbal almost laughed out loud at such a foolish idea, but he maintained his composure and asked, "What is your name?"

"Ramu is my name," the man answered.

"Ramu, you are just the man I am looking for," Birbal said with a smile, "would you please follow me?"

Without giving it a second thought, Ramu began following Birbal and the other two men still carrying the bundle of firewood on his head.

Birbal had now found three of the most foolish men of Delhi, and began searching for a fourth. But search as he may, he could not find anyone. When night fell, Birbal was still searching. Then suddenly, he saw a man practically bent over searching for something under a street lamp.

Birbal approached the man and asked, "What are you looking for?"

"I have lost a diamond ring somewhere in the darkness!" answered the man. But while he said this, he was pointing at some distant spot away from where he was standing.

"But why are you looking here," Birbal asked in surprise, "if, as you say, you have lost the ring over there?"

"Because the light is here and not there," answered the man somewhat incredulous at such a question.

"Oh I see," Birbal said, as if understanding completely. "If you will come with me," he told the man, "I will help you find your ring."

The man agreed and followed Birbal and the others. They soon arrived at the palace gates and Birbal went inside, followed by the four foolish men. Arriving before the king, Birbal

154

announced, "Your Majesty, I have brought you four of Delhi's most foolish men."

"Is that so?" asked Akbar in an amused tone. "And how did you conclude that they were the most foolish?" the king asked with curiosity.

"Why, by their actions, Your Majesty," answered Birbal with a smile.

He then recounted each of their peculiar actions. And when he had finished, Akbar said, "You have done well, Birbal. But, did I not ask you to bring six of the most foolish men? I see you have brought only four," the king said with a twinkle in his eyes, thinking that he had finally managed to trap Birbal. "Obviously you were not able to find two more foolish men," Akbar teased playfully.

"That is not true," answered Birbal calmly. "If Your Majesty will look carefully, you will indeed see six of Delhi's most foolish men standing here."

"What do you mean?" asked the king in surprise.

"Your Majesty," Birbal continued, "these four, plus you and I, make six. You, because you gave me such a foolish task. And I, because I foolishly carried it out."

Akbar burst out laughing and could only say, "Yes, Birbal. So I see, so I see!"

The Guru's Magic Stick

There once lived a Guru who had a magic stick. Whatever he touched with it turned into gold. It often happened that when he would go on his walks around the ashram, he would inadvertently touch something which would immediately turn into gold. When he went into the kitchen, he would sometimes stir the food with the magic stick, and the pots would turn into gold.

Now one day, a new disciple who had just recently come to stay at the ashram happened to witness this wonderful feat. Because he had always been poor, the greedy disciple one day decided to make his move. In the dead of night, he made his way into the kitchen and stole all the pots which had been turned into gold and left the ashram.

The next morning, the cook frantically ran to the Guru to report the theft. But the Guru appeared unconcerned. Instead, he lamented the bad luck of the thief saying, "That poor fool, instead of stealing the magic stick, he was contended to steal only a few pots and not the power which turned them into gold."

Such is our condition. We should not be contended with just superficial accomplishments, but should try and extract from the Guru that most precious of all gifts. That is, the awakening of our inner spiritual power, which will transform our lives.

Become Completely Absorbed In God

O nce a powerful king went to the forest to hunt. Being a pious *Muslim*, when the time came for his *namaz*—the daily prayer—he spread out his prayer rug and began to perform the afternoon prayer.

Meanwhile a young woman had set out in search of her husband who had gone to the forest early that day to gather firewood. When he had not returned at the appointed time, she became worried and set out to find him. She was so absorbed in thinking of her husband that she was not aware of anything else. Moving in the direction where her husband had gone, she accidentally stepped on the king's prayer rug.

When he saw this, the king became enraged. However, as one cannot speak during *namaz* the king remained silent. And, as she was not aware of what had happened, the girl continued on her way.

After finishing his prayers, the king was rolling up the rug when he noticed both the girl and her husband coming his way. When he saw the woman, he began shouting at her saying, "Don't you know that I am the ruler of India. You walked right over my prayer rug while I was doing my prayers."

"Your Majesty," the woman said humbly, "please forgive me. I was so absorbed in the thought of my husband that I was not aware of having walked over your prayer rug." "However," she added, "it is surprising to me that although you were supposed to be absorbed in worship, yet you noticed me stepping on your rug. I did not notice it as I was absorbed in my husband, a mere mortal, but you were praying to the Almighty!"

When we meditate, we should become completely absorbed in the object of our meditation. Just as the woman was lost in her love for her husband, we should lose ourselves in deep meditation and love for the Almighty.

The Descent of the River Ganga

Long ago there lived a great monarch in northern India named Sagara. He had conquered many of the neighboring kingdoms. His spiritual master now instructed him to perform the great horse sacrifice. In this sacrifice, a horse is released and is made to wander as he wishes throughout the land, thereby crossing many different kingdoms. If the horse's passage was obstructed in any way, particularly by military force, there would be an immediate battle with those protecting the horse. This would be considered a direct challenge to the sovereignty of the monarch.

Now it so happened that Indra, the king of the gods, decided to abduct the horse in order to frustrate the sacrifice. He decided to hide the horse in an underground cavern.

Upon hearing of the disappearance, the monarch sent his many sons in search of the horse. Some traveled east, some west, while the others north and south. Unable to locate the horse anywhere on land, they began searching for him underground, until finally he was located in an underground cave. He was standing near the great sage Kapila, who with eyes closed was engrossed in deep meditation.

The sons of Sagara immediately assumed that the sage had stolen the horse and wishing to kill him, they ran to attack him with raised swords. But the very moment they were about to strike, the sage made the sound of the seed *mantra* "*hum*" and instantly all of Sagara's sons were burnt to ashes.

After sometime, seeing that his sons did not return, the king sent his grandson Amshuman to search for them. Amshuman was an intelligent and kind hearted man, as well as being very dear to his grandfather. After searching for some time, he finally arrived at the scene. He noticed the sage sitting in meditation and the horse grazing nearby. But he could not understand what the pile of ashes all around the sage was.

Intuitively he recognized the greatness of the sage and humbly addressed him with great reverence. He requested the return of the horse and also inquired if the sage had seen his uncles. The sage was pleased with the boys respect and gave him permission to take the horse. "But as far as your uncles," the sage said, "only the purifying waters of the celestial river Ganga can resurrect them."

After being instructed on how to achieve such a feat by the sage, Amshuman returned with the horse to his grandfather, the monarch. Although the king completed the sacrifice, after it was over, he decided to retire to the forest after hearing about the death of all his children. He turned over the kingdom to Amshuman. Amshuman turned it over to his son Dilipa, so he could dedicate himself to performing the specific austerities needed to bring down to earth the cosmic river. However he was unsuccessful, and in due course of time he passed away. His son Dilipa decided to continue with the austerities himself, but he too died before the task was completed.

Now Dilipa had a son named Bhagiratha, and he decided

to take up the task. After performing severe austerities and practicing deep concentration, the goddess Ganga manifested herself to him and said, "I am pleased with your penance, and I shall fulfill your desire by descending to the earth. But who is there who can sustain the force of my descent? The force of my water will penetrate the very crust of the earth passing through to the subterranean region." "There is another problem which has to be resolved," continued the goddess. "When I flow over the earth, all of humanity will want to wash their sins in my sacred water. How will I purify myself from all those sins?" she asked.

As he listened to her concerns, Bhagiratha assured her that her waters would remain pure by the constant bathing of those great beings who have renounced all worldly desires, and who have controlled their senses. "By the contact of their bodies with your waters" he assured her, "all impurities will be absolved." "And regarding your descent," Bhagiratha continued, "I will propitiate Lord Shiva, who is the Self of all, and who is always concerned with the welfare of the world. I am sure he will agree to bear the force of your descent."

Hearing Bhagiratha's response, Mother Ganga urged him to propitiate Shiva without delay. After performing penance for some time, Lord Shiva became pleased and agreed to receive the celestial river on his head. As the Ganga reached the earth, Bhagiratha led the way in his chariot. He led her to the spot where the ashes of his fore-fathers lay. The moment her sacred water touched the ashes, they were released from their sins. By the mere contact of the water with the ashes, their spirits were set free. And to this day, its purifying water gives solace to millions of pilgrims each year.

161

The Sealed Box

In ancient times, a disciple was tested again and again by his Guru. When the seeker Hussein first went to meet the great Dul-il-Nul to offer himself as a disciple, the Master simply told him to sit down, and without uttering another word put him to work.

A year passed and the Guru called Hussein one day and asked him, "Where have you come from?"

"I came from *Rai*," answered Hussein.

After having asked him the single question, the Master motioned Hussein back to his work. Another year passed, and once again the Guru called Hussein. But this time, he called him closer to him and asked, "Why have you come?"

"I have come for your blessings," answered Hussein. The Master shook his head as if to say very good, but said nothing else. He again motioned Hussein to return to his work.

After the third year, the Master again called Hussein to himself and asked, "Hussein, what do want?"

"I want the secret *mantra*, and your divine spiritual touch," answered Hussein.

The Guru again nodded his head in agreement, but he then gave Hussein a small sealed box, which he placed in a basket. He told Hussein to take the basket and box to the other side of the river where a great being was living. "Go to him," said the Master, "and give him this box. He will give you everything."

Hussein took the basket and started out. But when he got to the river, he heard a noise coming from inside the box. His curiosity got the best of him, and he decided to open the box. Inside there was a small mouse, who immediately escaped into the forest. Hussein was now dejected and did not know if he should continue or return to the Master. He decided to go on and arrived at the *Mahatma's* hut. The old saint was very stern and was holding a stick in his hand.

Hussein approached the great being and said, "I have come from *Mahatma* Dul-il-Nul. He had given me a mouse to give to you, which was in this box, but unfortunately I opened it and he escaped."

The Mahatma became very angry and raising his stick at Hussein he shouted, "Get out of here! If you can't even take care of a tiny mouse, how can you repeat a great *mantra*?"

Hussein returned to Dul-il-Nul and holding the basket and empty box, he explained everything that had happened.

"Don't worry," the Master said, "it is obviously not yet your time. Return to your home, and if after twelve years you have not yet found someone, you can come back to me. In the meantime, do some spiritual practices."

This story illustrates the need for sincerity and obedience to the master's instructions. What the Master has to offer is extremely valuable, and before it can be entrusted to any one, the disciple must be worthy.

Emperor Akbar

Akbar was sincerely religious and an earnest seeker of truth. He ascended the Moghul throne at the age of thirteen. And from the age of nineteen, he made an annual pilgrimage to the burial shrine of the great sufi saint, Sheikh Mu'in-ud-din Chishti at Ajmeer. His court was opened to *faqirs, yogis,* Buddhist monks and Jains, even Jesuit priests. In fact, he loved the company of all great scholars, philosophers and saints. He himself was known to have had a number of mystical experiences, the first one recorded is said to have occurred when he was fifteen. According to Abu-'l-Fazl, it occurred during the siege of Mankot. Suddenly, Akbar experienced a mystical ecstasy and had to break away from the camp. He went to a nearby forest and remained in solitary meditation for many hours.

But although Akbar tried to be tolerant towards all religious views, many of those around him were violently intolerant. There were differences between Muslim and Hindus, and the Portuguese were against both Hindus and Muslims. There was an even more bitter rivalry between the two Muslim groups, the Sunnis and Shias.

All these differences disgusted Akbar. And his own beliefs alienated him from orthodox Islam. Although he was a Muslim by birth, by about the age of thirty-five, he went so far as to express his abhorrence of eating meat. A few months later, after ten days of preparation for a large hunting expedition, where all types of animals within a fifty mile circumference were to be rounded up and slaughtered, Akbar suddenly stopped the hunt and set all the animals free. A powerful spiritual mood is said to have overpowered him and after setting the animals free, he distributed alms and gold to all the *faqirs*.

To commemorate the inner call he had experienced, a structure was raised at the hallowed spot where he had sat. The area was then transformed into a beautiful and peaceful garden. By the end of the year, the house of worship which Akbar had built earlier was turned into a Parliament of Religions. There, philosophers, yogis, Sufis, Sunni and Shia, Brahmins, Sikhs, Buddhists, Jains, Christians, Jews, Zoroastrians, and any other believer, as well as atheists, were welcome to meet each other and discuss their beliefs in a spirit of tolerance.

The Swan and the Owl

Once a swan had been flying for sometime and becoming tired, landed on a nearby tree. Now this tree was the residence of the night bird, the owl. When the swan noticed the owl, he greeted him and said, "O brother owl, it is now midday and the bright sun has reached its zenith, I am so hot and tired that I have taken rest on this branch."

"What are you saying?" snapped back the sleepy owl sarcastically. "Are you trying to make a fool out of me?" he asked. "In all my life, I have never heard of such a thing," continued the owl. "My father, and his father before him never said such a thing either. The existence of a sun!" mumbled the owl to himself. "Whoever heard of such a thing? And its also supposed to create heat as well as give light to people. It does not get hot from sunlight," the owl assured the swan. "What actually occurs is that darkness thickens, and when its the most thickest, it then gives off the most heat."

"No, no, brother," the swan replied in disbelief, "It is not like that, you don't get heat from darkness, you get it from the sun's light. I can see this with my own eyes. It is such a divine sight. The sun is giving light to the whole world. How can you say that it doesn't?"

"Yes," lamented the owl, "there are plenty of you who pretend to know something and go around just to deceive others with such ideas." "Come," said the owl, "let us fly to those trees over there. I have many relatives living there. We will ask them whether what you say is true."

The two birds flew to the other trees where there were hundreds of owls. The owl gathered all the other owls around them and announced, "This fellow claims that there is some divine light which he calls the 'sun'. And he says that because it is now midday, this 'sun' is shining brightly, and it is giving off a lot of heat. Have you ever heard or seen such a thing?" asked the owl of his fellow owls.

"No, no, never" all the owls shouted in unison. "There are so many of us and not one has ever seen such a thing. Even our ancestors have never mentioned such a thing. This fool is trying to deceive us with such ridiculous claims."

"Let us take a vote," shouted one of the owls. And so they did, and every one of them said that there was no such thing as a sun. Soon they started to attack the swan, but fortunately he was able to escape.

This was one of my Guru's favorite stories. He liked it so much that he would often say that it had become like a mantra for him. In Indian symbolism the owl represents darkness or ignorance, while the swan symbolizes light and knowledge. The night loving owl cannot recognize the light of day no matter how much it is argued. Similarly, one who has not seen the light of the Spirit will naturally believe it does not exist. What is day for the swan is night for the owl, while what is night for the owl is day for the swan. Baba would often tell this story to show how religious orthodoxy arises out of ignorance of the truth. An enlightened sage makes the pronouncement "I am God." But their followers do not bother to make the effort to attain the same experience for themselves, and instead go around denying the truth that the Divine dwells within the heart. And the fact is, if you cannot find God within, you will not be able to find Him anywhere.

Nasrudin the Religious Teacher

Once Sheikh Nasrudin decided to give religious instructions. At the time he was sitting in a coffee shop and during the course of his lecture he said, "It is a great sin to smoke cigarettes, so don't smoke. Don't drink alcohol, that too is very bad." He continued his instructions with other do's and don'ts. "Reform yourselves," he admonished.

As is the custom, after the lecture there was a question and answer period, and a man asked, "Nasrudin, is that a packet of cigarettes in your pocket?"

"Oh yes," said Nasrudin, "I enjoy smoking."

"And," continued the man, "didn't I see you the other day sitting opposite me in the liquor shop drinking brandy?"

"I do drink," answered Nasrudin.

"Then why," asked the man, "are you giving a lecture asking people to give up such habits as you yourself engage in?"

"Oh brother," replied Nasrudin, "these lectures are for the benefit of others. I myself don't accept any knowledge."

As my Baba would say, "So don't be like Sheikh Nasrudin." You should practice what you preach.

170

The Procession of Ants

Many ages ago, the cosmic waters had been taken captive by the demon Vritra. This demon manifested himself in the limitless shape of a cosmic cloud. In this way, he kept the life giving waters from circulating freely throughout the universe for ages. The gods, as well as all life, suffered greatly during that period. But finally, Indra, the king of the gods became inspired to throw his weapon the thunderbolt at the demon. This is such a powerful weapon that the moment it struck the demon, it shattered, and the captive water burst free. As the cosmic waters were once again free, the demons retreated to the lower regions.

After returning to their respective heavenly region, however, Indra noticed how the once beautiful mansions had cracked and crumbled after such a long period of neglect. Because of this great victory, Indra, who was now being hailed as a savior by all the divinities decided to rebuild the ruined city and particularly his own palace. He immediately called Vishvakarman, the celestial builder and architect. Due to his great genius, in only one year, he succeeded in building many beautiful mansions, with gardens, lakes, and delicate architectural styles.

However, as the work progressed, Indra's demands and visions of grandeur grew greater and greater. He wanted more pavilions added, along with ponds and pleasure groves. Whenever he arrived to appraise the work, he would instead envision something greater.

171

This of course began to frustrate Vishvakarman, and he decided to approach Lord Brahma the Creator, who lived at a higher region and was thereby above the petty ambitions, desires, and strife's of the divinities. Brahma listened with grand-fatherly understanding at Vishvakarman's troubles and comforted him. He assured him that he would soon be relieved of his burden and sent him home in peace.

As Vishvakarman traveled back down to Indra's city, Brahma traveled up to a higher sphere where lies Vishnu, the Supreme Being, of whom it is said that the Creator is but an agent. Coming before the silent and beatific Lord, Brahma recounted what Vishvakarman had told him. By a mere nod of the head, the Lord let it be known that He was aware of the situation and would soon fulfill Vishvakarman's request.

Early the next morning, a beautiful *brahmin* boy carrying a pilgrim's staff suddenly appeared at Indra's gate. The gatekeeper rushed to inform Indra of the exquisitely attractive boy who appeared to be about ten years of age. When Indra arrived at the gate, he noticed a crowd of enraptured children staring at the boy's radiant luster.

Upon seeing Indra, the boy greeted him with a gentle glance of his brilliant eyes. The king bowed to the holy child and the boy gave him his blessing. The king invited the boy into the palace hall, where he welcomed the mysterious visitor with oblations of honey, milk, and fruits. After welcoming him, Indra addressed the boy saying, "O Venerable Boy, please tell me the purpose of your visit."

With a deep and soft voice, the child said, "O king of the gods, I have heard of the magnificent palace you are building and have

172

come to relate to you the question which is in my mind. How many years will it take to complete this splendid and spacious residence?" "O highest of gods," continued the boy, "how many more feats of engineering will Vishvakarman have to perform? No Indra before you has ever succeeded in completing the kind of palace you crave."

He was inflated by the conceit of victory, so Indra was amused at the child's pretension to having knowledge of other Indras who lived many eons earlier than himself. With a fatherly smile he asked the boy, "Tell me child! Are there many Indras and Vishvakarmans whom you have seen, or at least, whom you have heard of?"

"Yes indeed," the child calmly nodded. "I have seen many." Although the young boy answered with a warm and sweet voice, the words sent a slow chill through Indra's veins.

"My dear child," the boy continued, "I knew your father, Kashyapa, who is the progenitor of all earthly creatures. And I knew your grandfather, Marichi, who was born of Brahma's pure spirit. I also know Brahma who is brought forth on a lotus growing out of Vishnu's naval. And Vishnu, the Supreme Being, Him too I know.

"O king of gods, I have known the dreadful dissolution of the universe. I have seen all perish, again and again, at the end of every cycle. At that time, every atom which makes up the universe is reabsorbed back into the fathomless and infinite ocean. No beings remain in that empty and utter darkness. Aah, who can count the universes that have passed away, or those creations yet to be. Who could number the endless ages of the world and count the infinite number of universes existing side by side, each containing its Brahma, its Vishnu, and its Rudra? Who will count the Indras in them all, let alone those who have passed away, and those yet to appear. All succeeding each other, ascending to godly kingship one by one, and one by one passing away? Some among your servants maintain that it may be possible to number the grains of sand on earth, or the drops of rain that fall from the sky, but no one will ever be able to count all those Indras. This is what the Knowers know."

"The life and kingship of an Indra lasts for 857,143 years, and when twenty-eight Indras have expired, only one day and night of Brahma has elapsed. The full age of one Brahma measured in such Brahma days and nights is one hundred and eight years. Brahma follows Brahma; one sinks, the next arises, in an endless series."

"In this way, innumerable universes exist simultaneously, each having its own Brahmas and Indras. Like delicate boats, they float on the fathomless pure waters that form Vishnu's body. Out of each hair-pore of that body a universe bubbles up and then breaks. Will you presume to count all of them? Can you number the gods in all those worlds, past and present?" the boy asked.

Meanwhile, while the boy was speaking, a procession of ants had made their way into the hall. In military array, a column over five yards wide paraded across the floor. As he noticed them, the boy paused and stared at them, then suddenly laughed out loud, but immediately withdrew into a thoughtful silence.

"Why do you laugh?" asked Indra in surprise. "Who are you mysterious being disguised in the guise of a boy?" The king's throat had become dry and his voice stammered.

174

"I laughed because of the ants," answered the boy. "But please don't ask me to give the reason. For within this secret is enclosed both woe and wisdom. It is this secret which strikes at the root of worldly vanity like an ax. This secret lies buried in the wisdom of the ages and is rarely revealed even to saints. To those who renounce and transcend mortal existence, this knowledge is bliss; but it destroys those who are full of desire and deluded by worldliness."

The boy smiled and then once again remained silent. Indra observed him for a moment. Then said with visible humility, "O son of Brahmin, I do not know who you are. You appear to be Wisdom Incarnate. Please reveal to me this secret of the ages, this light which dispels the dark."

Requested by Indra to be taught, the boy pointing to the parade of ants said, "Indras, one and all. Like you, each one of them, by virtue of pious deeds once ascended to the rank of a king of gods. But now, through many rebirths, each has again become an ant. This army is an army of former Indras. Through piety and good deeds, the inhabitants of the world become elevated to higher celestial regions; but by wicked deeds they sink back down to the worlds below, reincarnating as trees, insects, and other animals. It is one's deeds which gives happiness or sorrow. It is deeds that make one a master or a serf, a king or a brahmin, one of the gods, an Indra or Brahma. This is the essence of the secret. This wisdom carries one across the ocean of worldly existence."

After having said the above, the young boy suddenly disappeared. The king remained alone amazed at all that had occurred. Indra thought he had dreamed the events he had seen, but he no longer desired the splendor of his heavenly palace, nor its expansion. Calling Vishvakarman to the palace, he greeted his craftsman with love and appreciation. He showered on him many precious gifts and jewels. After a delightful dinner celebration, the cosmic architect was sent home.

Indra lost all interest in his kingdom and now desired only spiritual liberation. He entrusted the royal seat to his son and was about to retire to the forest, but on seeing him dressed as a hermit, his beautiful wife and queen, Shachi, became overcome with grief. Depressed and in utter despair, she ran to Brihaspati, the celestial priest and Guru of the gods.

Brihaspati, whose mystical powers helped restore the heavenly government of the universe from the control of the demons on many occasions welcomed the queen and comforted her. Then, taking her by the hand, he proceeded to the palace. When seeing the disinterested mood of the king, Brihaspati started speaking to Indra on the virtues of the spiritual life. But he also pointed out the value of the worldly and domestic life as well, giving equal importance to both. The skillful teacher shortly persuaded his disciple to give up his extreme resolve, and to carry on his duties as the king of the gods, along with his spiritual practices. Upon seeing her husband persuaded, Shachi was once again happy, and her exquisite radiance also returned.

So ends the story of how Indra, the king of the gods, who was humiliated and then cured of his great pride learned the lessons of life. Using the wisdom he had learnt and putting it to practice, he came to know of his proper role in the unending cosmic play. This story is related in the Brahmavaivarta Purana.

The Weight of Forty Years

There was once a great saint named Bulle Shah. For forty years, he is said to have studied different religions and all the available books of philosophy. He was even initiated into the spiritual life by many teachers, but still he never felt contended. On the contrary, all his learning had actually created more turmoil and doubts within his mind. All the information he had gathered from the various scriptures and the different techniques he had learned from all the teachers became a mental burden. Try as he would, he could neither benefit from his learning, nor could he bear its tremendous weight. He appeared like a man constantly wandering about with a heavy load of books on his head; indeed, it was like the weight of forty years.

Now one day, a friend came to visit him, but when he saw Bulle Shah's appearance, he was pained to find his friend so burdened with the weight of learning. "How are you brother?" asked the concerned friend.

"What can I say," answered Bulle Shah, "how can I describe my condition? I am carrying a great load, yet I don't know how to get rid of it."

The friend said, "Oh brother, there is a great saint in the city named Shah Inayat. Let us go and meet him. I am sure he can help you."

So they went to meet the great master, and when they reached the spot, Bulle Shah's friend said to the saint, "Sir, this man has studied all the different religions and philosophies, but it has now become a heavy mental burden, and he feels extremely unhappy. If you could help in removing some of this weight, he would be eternally grateful to you.

The saint looked into Bulle Shah's eyes and said, "Stay with me for a few days. But for the moment, leave aside the bundle of book knowledge you are carrying on your head."

Bulle Shah said that he would try and accepted the saint's invitation. Nothing happened for two days, but on the third day the master called Bulle Shah and touched him at the spot between the eyes. Suddenly, the heavy weight Bulle Shah had been carrying all those years appeared to dissolve. Just as a man carrying a heavy load feels immediate relief once he puts the bundle down, in the same way, Bulle Shah felt immediate relief.

Bulle Shah remained absorbed in this newly discovered inner peace for a number of hours. Afterward, Inayat Shah told him to return to his own home and continue to practice what he had given him. Now as time passed, Bulle Shah realized that true peace and joy was really inside himself. He, therefore, began to tell everyone that true joy and love could not be found in books, temples, mosques, or churches.

"There is no need to go to all these places," he would tell them, "just go within yourself. For forty years, I searched in books and other external places, yet I did not gain anything but fatigue."

Now of course, when the orthodox teachers heard this, they did not like it at all. They soon turned against Bulle Shah and even organized meetings to discuss what to do about him. They finally decided to use Islamic law against him by accusing him of blasphemy. A conference was organized and they summoned Bulle Shah.

"You speak against all religions and teachers," they said, "therefore you have committed a grave sin and must be punished for it."

"Well what is your punishment," asked Bulle Shah.

"Since there is no sin worse than heresy," they answered, "we have decided that your body should be branded with a hot iron bar in twenty different places."

""I'll accept the punishment," Bulle Shah said, "but may I ask you something?"

"Yes of course," replied the priests.

"If there is a wealthy man or teacher," said Bulle Shah, "and they tell an innocent man that if he would do what they told him, that he would be rewarded the next day, or the day after. Yet, even after one year passes, then two, then five, then ten, twenty, thirty and forty years, still he has not received what was promised to him. What, in your opinion?" asked Bulle Shah, "should be the punishment for such a teacher?"

"That indeed is a horrible crime," the assembly of teachers replied. "When one has nothing to give, yet he makes others work for him for nothing, then his body should be branded with the hot iron in at least twenty places as well."

"Do all of you agree?" asked Bulle Shah.

"Yes we do," answered the priests in unison.

"Very well," said Bulle Shah, "all of you are guilty of this crime. For forty years, you have made me study books, you have taught me different techniques and practices, with the promise of some great reward. Yet, after all these years, I had still not received that which you promised. Therefore, after you brand my body, be prepared to brand your own bodies as well."

Of course none of them were willing to have their own bodies branded. And out of guilt, they dismissed the charges against Bulle Shah. This is in fact the situation many find themselves in. You are told to study this book or that book. Go to this church, temple or mosque. But true spirituality can never be found in books or learning. It is something which can be found only by going within ourselves. And if we could meet such a rare saint as Bulle Shah had met, then by his blessings our attention would be directed within. Although the original founders of the different religions wished to reunite man with God, unfortunately such religions have been used as tools to tear them apart even further. God is not the exclusive property of any religion. He cannot be copyrighted by anyone, as my Guru would often say. He answers the call of the heart of anyone who calls with faith and devotion.

This World Is An Illusion

O nce the great sage Vasishtha was teaching his student Rama, "God is real, this world is an illusion!" Now one day, it so happened that they were walking together along a street when suddenly a commotion arose. People were running here and there shouting, "Get out of the way a mad elephant is running wild."

As Rama heard this, he recalled his Guru's instruction, "God is real, and the world is an illusion!" He therefore stood his ground without fear. As the elephant came closer, Vasishtha suddenly ran into the forest obviously anxious to get away from the raging elephant. Upon seeing this, Rama thought, "How do you like that? Here all this time Vasishtha has been teaching me that only God is real and everything else is an illusion, and yet when he is put to the test, he runs away like a frightened child?"

When the danger had passed, Rama approached his Guru and asked him why he had run away. "Had he forgotten his own teaching?" Rama asked.

"Not at all," the sage replied. "All this is indeed an illusion. The raging elephant is an illusion, people running in fear is an illusion, you standing firm is an illusion, and so is my running away an illusion as well."

Why There Are Eclipses

Once, ages ago, the gods and demons gathered together in order to churn the cosmic ocean for *amrita*, the nectar of immortality. They had agreed to work together with the condition that they would share the nectar between themselves.

Since the task was not going to be an easy one, it required the cooperation between these two naturally opposing forces. But after the work was done, and the nectar was found, the gods did not want to share it with their enemies. But now that the *amrita* had been found, how were they going to distribute it to the gods without giving any to the demons?

The gods approached Lord Vishnu with their problem. Vishnu decided to turn himself into a beautiful woman named Mohini. She was so captivating that everyone immediately fell in love with her the moment they saw her. It was announced that Mohini would distribute the nectar between the gods and demons. However, she had no intention of giving any to the demons, because if they became immortal, the cosmic order would become disturbed.

Mohini told the gods and demons to sit in two lines, and she would give each of them their share. But although she gave the gods the nectar, whenever she approached the demons, she would only pretend to give them some. By turning on her charms, she would distract the demons, thereby making them think that they were sharing in the nectar.

Now among the demons there was one named Rahu. Somehow he saw through Mohini's game and disguising himself as a *Deva*, he sat in the line of the gods. He sat between the Sun and Moon quietly waiting for his turn.

When it was his turn, Mohini gave Rahu some of the nectar. But the Sun and Moon were both suspicious of him and sounded the alarm. But it was too late, Rahu had already put the nectar into his mouth. However, he had not yet swallowed it, and Vishnu (Mohini) immediately threw his *chakra* weapon and severed the demon's head from his torso. But the damage had already been done. Since he had already tasted the nectar, he became immortal like the gods, but now his body was cut in two. The head portion continued to be known as Rahu, but the torso was called Ketu.

To this day, Rahu is known as the dragon's head to astrologers, while Ketu is its tail. Although these demons are invisible, they still exist and are filled with hatred towards the Sun and Moon for having revealed their identity. Because of this, whenever the Sun and Moon comes near their positions, the luminaries are swallowed by Rahu and Ketu, thereby creating darkness in the world. Sometimes the Sun is eclipsed, while at other times it is the Moon. This has continued without interruption ever since the gods and demons churned the cosmic ocean ages ago.

This is My Water-Bowl, This is My Yoga-Stick!

The great king Janaka used to leave his royal palace and travel to a secluded spot in the forest in order to practice meditation. He would sit on the banks of a river and continuously repeat: So'Ham, So'Ham, So'Ham - meaning "That am I, That am I, That am I."

Now it so happened that one day, Ashtavakra happened to pass by that way. Although just a young boy, Ashtavakra was a fully enlightened being. When the boy heard the king, he was surprised and thought to himself, "The king is supposed to be enlightened, yet he is sitting here repeating So'Ham, So'Ham, So'Ham like a parrot."

Ashtavakra approached the king and sat down right in front of him and holding his water-bowl in one hand, while resting his arm on his yoga-stick (*yogadanda*), he began repeating, "This is my water-bowl, this is my yoga-stick, this is my water-bowl, this is my yoga-stick, this is my water-bowl, this is my yoga-stick."

When he heard this commotion, the king opened his eyes and saw the young boy shouting right in front of him. He thought to himself, "I have left the noise and disturbances of the palace in order to seek a solitary spot to contemplate God, but even here I am disturbed."

Noticing that the king was becoming agitated, Ashtavakra began shouting even louder, "This is my water-bowl! This is my yoga-stick! This is my water-bowl! This is my yoga-stick!"

The king was now so frustrated that he stopped doing his practices and said, "Oh foolish child, what are you shouting? Who has told you that these are *not* your water-bowl and your yoga-stick?"

Ashtavakra snapped back, "Oh deluded king, what are you doing? Who has told you that you are *not* 'That', that you are not the highest Truth. What is the purpose of repeating 'That am I' over and over again like a parrot?"

Suddenly the veil of ignorance was lifted, and the king embraced the young boy saying, "Here I thought that you were a nuisance, but instead you have bestowed on me a great blessing."

The Self is always present within us. It has always been there and will always be there. In Vedantic philosophy, an important and subtle question is raised. Do we attain what we haven't got, or do we attain what we already have? If we attain something which we did not already have, there is every possibility that we will lose it at some point. If it did not already exist within us, it would not be real because something is real only if it exists at all times. Therefore, Vedanta says that there is nothing to be done. The most important thing is understanding. Through understanding comes liberation.

Whatever You Say

Once Emperor Akbar invited Birbal to the palace for dinner. One of the items was a cabbage recipe. After dinner the king asked, "Birbal, what did you think of the cabbage dish?"

"I thought it was delicious," Birbal said.

"I thought it tasted awful," scoffed the king.

"Your right, Your Majesty," Birbal said, "it tasted quite bland."

"But you just said that it tasted delicious," the king replied in surprise.

"Yes," Birbal said, "but I am the servant of His majesty, not the cabbage."

The Word of a Donkey

One day a neighbor called on Mullah Nasrudin and said, "Oh Nasrudin, would you lend me your donkey today? I need to transport some goods to the next town."

Nasrudin was not inclined to lend his donkey to this particular neighbor and so not to be rude said, "I'm sorry, but I have already lent him to someone else."

But the moment he said this, the sound of the donkey braying could be heard coming from behind the wall in Nasrudin's stable.

"How can you say that?" the neighbor asked in disbelief, "I can hear him braying just behind that wall."

"I am surprised at you," the Mullah said in indignation, "You would take the word of a donkey over the word of a respectable Sheikh as myself?"

Ajamila

It is believed that if a person commits sinful acts and does not repent and expedites its fruits in this life, the penalty will have to be paid in the next life. However, the suffering is then said to be greater. But if a person continues to commit sinful deeds, even after many acts of expiation, such repentance will have no effect. By developing love for God, however, and repeating his holy name, such devotion can lead to the highest good. Even death can be conquered by such love and surrender to the Almighty. To illustrate this, an ancient story is told about how Ajamila overcame death.

Ajamila, a *brahmin* by birth, married a woman who belonged to a lower caste than himself. She had a criminal nature and so influenced Ajamila. Soon he too became dishonest. But Ajamila had ten sons, and the youngest Narayana, who was named after God, was his favorite. After many years of dishonest living, Ajamila lay on his death bed. As his awareness moved from this world to the next, he saw three hideous demons approaching him at a distance. They were the attendance of Yama, the king of the dead coming to take his soul from his body.

Being stricken with terror, Ajamila called out to his son Narayana. But as he did so, his mind became concentrated on the Lord. The moment this occurred, the attendants of Lord Vishnu (Narayana) came before him and stood guard protecting him against Yama's attendants. When he saw the

Lord's attendants blocking their way, the demons asked, "Why do you protect this man and stop the natural course of events? You know the cosmic law of cause and effect. The course of one's future life is determined by their past actions. We, who are the attendants of Yama, know the past, present, and future of all souls. We are here to obey this cosmic law and make sure this person gets his just rewards."

"This Ajamila was a good man in his youth. He was self controlled, truthful, friendly towards all, and pure. He also was well versed in the scriptures. One day Ajamila happened to be in the woods picking flowers for his daily worship, but while there he noticed a young man and woman engaged in amorous acts. Suddenly Ajamila became infatuated with the girl and even left his lawful wife to be with her. The girl was a greedy and dishonest person and made Ajamila waste his entire fortune trying to please her. When his wealth was gone, he too started earning a living by dishonest means. Now he must pay for his evil deeds, so kindly move aside," they demanded.

But Vishnu's attendants replied, "This man has expiated all of his sins by uttering the Lord's divine name, and surrendering himself to Him. Yes, the mere name of God has the power to save even the most depraved man. It is God's love which purifies the mind. It can not be eradicated by mere expiation alone, especially if one continues performing evil deeds."

Upon hearing their response, Yama's attendants left that place in submission to the Lord's attendants. As they left, Ajamila regained consciousness. He could still see the Lord's angels, but soon they also disappeared from his vision. Gradually his health returned back to normal, but Ajamila was a changed man.

"Although I have lived a very wicked life," he thought to himself, "yet through the Lord's infinite mercy, I have been granted the vision of his attendants. This is indeed a great blessing. I feel that I am now purified. My whole life seems transformed."

From that day onwards, Ajamila performed only good deeds. He left his wicked wife and went to live on the banks of the river Ganga to practice *yoga*. He practiced meditation and chanting for many years until finally his mind became steady, and was firmly fixed in the thought of God. But at last, death once again approached Ajamila. Once more he saw the Lord's attendants coming to him. This time he prostrated himself before them and then meditated on the Lord giving up his body. Beckoned by the Lord's attendants, Ajamila entered their celestial vehicle, and was taken to the Lord's abode.

The Scriptures
Are the Form of God

There was once a pious *brahmin* living in the sacred city of Jagannatha Puri who was deeply devoted to Lord Krishna and recited the Bhagavad Gita every day. Since he was completely preoccupied in this way and had no other means of income, his finances started dwindling. He was soon reduced to poverty, and because of this, he and his family had to fast for a number of days.

On the third day, while reading the Gita as usual, he came across the following verse in the ninth chapter which read: "I shall supply all the needs of my devotees who are always immersed in me."

Reading this verse, he suddenly stopped and began to doubt the truth of these words. He underlined the verse in red ink and thought to himself, "Although God promises to take care of His devotees, still I have had to fast for three days despite my many years of devotion. I wonder why this is?"

Meanwhile, as he was thinking in this way, a young handsome boy approached his wife carrying a bag full of groceries. He handed them over to the brahmin's wife. He then asked her to prepare a meal for her family. Now the wife was so attracted by the boy, that she invited him to stay and eat with them. The boy agreed, and after preparing the meal, she asked him to go call her husband. The boy went to the spot where the brahmin was reading the Gita and told him that his wife was calling him for lunch.

As the brahmin got up, he noticed a scratch on the boy's arm which was bleeding and asked what had happened. The boy replied, "It is a scratch caused by the line you made in the Gita." Suddenly the brahmin recognized who the boy was. Being overwhelmed by remorse, he fainted on the spot. When he came to, the boy had vanished.

Therefore, the story teller says that the scriptures should be considered as the very form of God. And it is only when they are regarded in this way that we will gain the knowledge contained in them.

The Cat Ate It!

One day Nasrudin gave his wife some meat to cook for his dinner. He told his wife, "Prepare this piece of meat the way I like it, and we will enjoy it this evening when I return."

Nasrudin then went to perform some errands. Now it so happened that a friend of his wife came to visit and she wanted to offer her friend some of the meat. But by the time her friend had left, they had finished all of the meat.

Now that evening, when Nasrudin sat down for his dinner, the meal arrived, but there was no meat.

"Where is the meat which I gave you this morning?" asked the Mullah.

"The cat ate it," replied his wife.

"All three pounds of it?" asked Nasrudin in surprise.

"Yes," said his wife evasively.

Nasrudin picked up a pair of scales and weighed the cat. The cat also happened to weigh three pounds.

"If this is the cat," said Nasrudin, "where is the meat? And, if on the other hand this is the meat, then where is the cat?"

The Value of a Saints' Company

Once, when Narada visited heaven he saw God quietly meditating. "What is the Lord doing?" Narada asked one of the Lord's attendants. "He is doing his daily worship." the attendant answered. "What?" Narada exclaimed in surprise. "The whole universe worships God," Narada said, "so who could He be worshipping?"

Narada waited patiently until the Lord finished his worship. When it was over, Narada asked, "Lord, I asked your servant what you were doing and he told me that you were worshipping. Do you also have to worship?"

"Oh yes!" answered the Lord, "Everyone has to do worship."

This completely surprised Narada and he asked, "Lord, please tell me who is your God?"

The Lord replied, "My object of worship is the holy feet of saints."

This completely surprised Narada and he asked, "Lord, please tell me what is the effect of seeing a saint and living with him for some time?"

With a smile on his lips, the Lord said, "Narada, I can not answer this question because only one who has had a first hand experience of it can tell you." "However," the Lord continued, "I can guide you to one who will answer your question."

So the Lord sent Narada to a certain field where he would see a large dung heap, in which there lived a black beetle. "Ask him your question," the Lord told Narada, "and he will answer it."

Narada went to the distant field and found the dung heap described by the Lord. Calling the black beetle out of the heap of dung, Narada put his question to him. But before he could complete the question, the beetle suddenly fell over and died. Surprised at the turn of events, Narada returned to heaven and related to the Lord what had occurred.

Vishnu said, "I'm sorry for what has happened Narada, but if you go to a certain lake in the Himalayas, you will find a swan sitting on its shore. If you ask him your question, he will answer it."

Narada immediately went to the lake and saw the swan. He bowed to the swan and said, "I have been sent here by the Lord to whom I had put a question. My question was, 'What is the effect of seeing a saint for a short moment, and the effect of living with him?' Can you answer this question?" asked Narada.

Now the moment the swan heard Narada's question, he began to violently flap his wings and suddenly fell over dead. Narada became very perplexed at the situation and wondered why the swan died so suddenly?

Narada immediately returned to heaven and told the Lord what had happened. "I still can not answer your question," said the Lord, "but if you go to a certain kingdom, you will find that the king has been blessed with a son just three days old. Ask that child, and he will answer your question."

Narada traveled to the kingdom which the Lord had described, and met the king. He told the king, "Your Majesty, I have been sent here by the Lord. I have been told that you have a new son. Please take me to him so that I may ask him a question."

Now all the courtiers were amused at Narada's idea that such a small child could answer his question. And although the king was also perplexed he said, "O Narada, you are a great saint, you must certainly know what you are doing." So the king took him to the child's room.

The baby, being so young, was naturally lying on his back in the crib. Narada greeted the child and paid his respect to him. Then he asked his question. Immediately the child stood up and began to emit a beautiful light. He also acquired the power of speech and soon appeared to become transformed right before everyone's eyes into a most fascinating deity. Suddenly, he began to speak to Narada saying, "You are indeed most welcomed here O great sage. It is indeed by your blessings alone that I have attained my present state. I am so grateful to you. As a result of my past bad actions, I was born as a beetle living in a heap of elephant dung. But the moment I saw you, I was released from my suffering. I again took birth and was born a swan living high in the Himalayas. I again had the good fortune of your holy sight (*darshan*). And I was freed from the conditions of that life. I next took birth as a prince, and again I had your darshan. Now, by your holy sight, I have been transformed into a divine being."

And so Narada's question on the value of a saint's company was answered. When such brief encounters can effect the direction of one's destiny, one can only imagine the benefits of living with such a great being for some time.

The Story of Eknath

The great 16th Century Maharashtrian saint Eknath had a desire for self-realization from his early youth. He knew the importance of a Guru, so Eknath went in search of one. He heard that there was a great saint named Janardan Swami living in the fortress at Devagiri.

The young seeker walked the forty or fifty mile distance and asked the great Guru if he could serve him, thereby following the scriptural injunction which says that one who desires knowledge should serve a spiritual master. The Guru accepted him and Eknath began serving him in earnest. He began to reduce his sleep and comforts getting up before his teacher and going to sleep after his teacher. He also took his meals only after his Guru had taken his.

One day, the Guru decided to test Eknath to see if he was ripe for spiritual knowledge. So he asked him to do the ashram accounts. Eknath did the accounts until late into the night, but he could not balance the books. He went over it again and again but could not account for a penny. He stayed up the whole night working on the problem. The next morning, when his Guru got up, he saw Eknath dancing around the room.

"What is this?" asked Janardan, "why are you so happy?"

"I have found the missing penny, I found the missing penny!"

shouted Eknath happily. "I went over the accounts a thousand times during the night but could not find that missing penny. But just now I found the mistake."

Janardan was pleased with the dedication and persistence of his disciple and said, "Now I want you to concentrate your mind in the same way on the Lord. Only by doing so will you attain the highest good." Janardan said no more, but he placed his hand on his disciples head in blessing.

This is the kind of devotion a seeker must have when serving the Guru. One who serves the master with such dedication and sincerity will attain Self-Realization in a short time. The master can't help but be pleased and will bless such a worthy disciple in no time.

What If It's True?

Once Mullah Nasrudin was walking through town when the local children decided to tease him. They began following him. Some of the boys made fun of him by making strange jesters whenever his back was turned. Then everyone would laugh.

The Mullah decided to distract them by saying: "There is a big party being held at the home of a well known lawyer. And they are distributing cake, ice-cream, and candy to all the children. Why are you here? You should be at the party!"

Upon hearing this, the children became excited and ran towards the lawyer's home.

The Mullah was satisfied, and smiled to himself at his ingenuity. But then he thought, "What if it's true and there really is a party at the lawyer's home?" And with that the Mullah began to run towards the lawyer's house along with the children.

The Problem With A Little Knowledge

Once a student who had studied some books on Vedanta visited a well known Guru. Trying to impress the master, he began rattling off some principles of non-dualistic Vedanta saying, "There is no mind, no body, no world. One thing is not good and another bad. There is no guru and no disciple. All these things do not really exist but only appear to do so due to the elusive power of Maya."

All along the master had been sitting quietly listening to the boy. Then suddenly he picked up his staff and whacked the young man across the back. The boy suddenly jumped up from the pain of the blow and yelled in anger, "What do you think you're doing you foolish old man?"

"If nothing exists, or is real," the master asked, "then where does your anger come from?"

Setting Fire To Heaven

O nce Shibli, a disciple of the great Mansur was walking down one of the streets near the Ka'ba in Mecca— Islam's most sacred spot. He was carrying a torch and was in an unusual state. He appeared to be angry and had an intense look on his face.

"Where are you going?" asked many who saw him.

"I am going to set fire to heaven. I am going to set fire to the joy of heaven, and I am going to extinguish the fire of hell. I am going to smash the sacred stone in the Ka'ba."

"What are you saying?" shouted the crowd in anger, "You are going to destroy the sacred stone in the Ka'ba?"

"Don't you understand?" asked Shibli. "If I set fire to heaven, and if I extinguish the fire of hell, and if I break the stone in the Ka'ba, then people will look within their own hearts, where they will find God dwelling."

The Two Sisters

There once lived two sisters, each living on two separate hills. One of the hills was made of sugar, while the other was a salt hill. On the hill of salt, there was nothing but salt; while on the sugar hill, there was nothing but sugar.

Now the sisters had not seen each other for a long time but once they happened to meet unexpectedly. The sister who lived on the sugar hill appeared radiant and happy, but the one from the salt hill looked exhausted and pale.

The shriveled one asked her older sister, "What is the secret of your wonderful glow? What have you been eating?"

"I live on a hill made of sugar, and I eat a lot of it," answered the sister. "I live cheerfully and don't worry very much. Perhaps that is the reason for my happiness. But why do you look so sad and sickly?" she asked her sister.

"I live on a hill made of salt," answered the younger sister, "and I don't feel enthusiasm for anything. I always feel tired and weak."

The healthy sister said, "Come to my place and stay for sometime as my guest. I am sure that you will become healthy and happy in no time."

The younger sister agreed but said she could not come right away as she had to return to her place and attend to a number of things. Finally she was ready to go, but before she left, she made a large salt cake and took it with her to her sister's house.

When she arrived, her older sister welcomed her warmly and said, "My home is your home. Consider everything as belonging to you and live happily here."

She then got busy with her own work. The elder sister continued to eat sugar while the younger one ate the salt cake she had brought with her. After about two weeks, the younger sister said, "I have been here all this time but have not gained a single pound of weight."

"What have you been eating?" asked the elder sister.

"I have been eating the salt cake which I brought with me," answered the younger sister.

"How do you expect to gain any weight if you don't eat the sugar here?" asked the elder sister. "With so much sugar all around, what prevents you from eating sugar. While you are here, you should eat nothing but sugar."

"What can I do?" asked the younger sister, "My time here is over and I have to return to my own home."

"Don't worry," said the elder sister, "I know exactly what to do."

She made her sister a large sugar cake and said, "Now eat only this cake during your journey home, it will certainly benefit you, and when you have time you can visit me again."

The younger sister started eating only the sugar cake, and within a few days she became like a different person. Her attitude improved, and as the food suited her system very well, she also began to glow with radiance.

It is indeed our attitude towards life and the benefits of living in a good environment which gives contentment and inner peace. We will also find it beneficial if we keep the company of saintly people.

The King's Shoes

The Moghul Emperor Akbar had a deep interest in all religions. Religious leaders would gather in his court and argue the merits and demerits of various spiritual doctrines. One day, the discussion was centered around the value of holy places of pilgrimage.

Birbal, who was the king's wise counselor, decided to teach the king a practical lesson. He took a pair of the king's shoes and buried them at a certain spot. He then started circumambulating the mound at regular times of the day.

This soon attracted the interest of some local people, who thought that it must be a holy spot, and so they too started walking around it and offering prayers.

Soon, due to the intensity of their faith, some of their prayers were answered. These grateful devotees decided to build a small shrine over the mound, and it soon became well known as a sacred place. Pilgrims began visiting the spot from distant places and soon reports reached Akbar who decided to visit the sight himself. He asked Birbal to accompany him, and when they arrived seeing everyone bowing reverently at the shrine, the king wondered about it and asked, "Birbal, is this the resting place of some great saint?"

"No, your Majesty," Birbal answered with a smile, "it is only the resting place of your shoes."

Surprised at Birbal's answer, he asked his minister what he meant. So Birbal explained to the king the whole story of how he had buried the king's shoes. Having knowledge of human nature, and realizing the power of faith, Birbal explained to the king how the human mind works by giving him a practical experience of it. Akbar became very pleased with his wise minister's lesson.

The Dispute Between
The Physical Organs

O nce a dispute arose among the various physical organs of the body. Not able to agree on who was the greatest among themselves, they approached Prajapati, the creator and asked, "Which of us is the best?"

"That one among you who on departing your company people consider the physical body as simply a corpse, that one is considered the best."

So first, the organ of speech left the company of the other organs of the body for a whole year. When he returned he inquired, "How did you manage to live without me?"

"We lived just as dumb people do," answered the other organs, "we simply did not speak through the instrument of speech. But through the life force, we saw through the eyes, heard through the ears, knew through the mind, and had children through the organ of regeneration."

Next the eyes went out, leaving his companions behind. After staying away for a year they returned and asked, "How did you manage to live without us?"

The other organs said, "We lived just as blind people do, without seeing through the eyes. But through the vital force, we spoke through the organ of speech, heard through the ear, knew through the mind, and had children through the organ of regeneration."

In this way, each of the remaining organs; the ear; the mind; the organ of regeneration, each left the company of the others for one year, and when they returned found that the others continued to exist without any difficulty.

Finally, the vital force, known as *prana*, was about to go out, and by its very action, suddenly the other organs became uprooted. Realizing what was happening, they all chimed in unison, "Wait, please don't go out, we can not live without you."

"All right," said the vital force, "since you have realized my greatness I will stay."

Therefore, the vital force was praised and recognized as the most important element in the physical body.

The Woodcutter and His Ax

There was once a woodcutter. One day, while cutting wood, his ax fell over and became hidden underneath the pile of wood. A local boy used to visit him daily just to watch him work. But when the man could not find his ax, he became suspicious of the boy and thought to himself, "This boy must have stolen my ax."

The next day when the boy visited the woodcutter, the man looked at the boy's face and thought to himself, "His face appears to be that of a thief. I am certain he has stolen the ax."

Now the boy was exactly as he had always been. But the woodcutter's outlook was different. He called to the boy and asked, "Look, I know that you have stolen my ax, so please bring it back."

"I didn't steal your ax, nor have I seen it," replied the boy.

"When I look at your face," said the woodcutter, "it tells me you have stolen my ax. Your eyes also tell me that you have stolen it."

"What do you mean by that?" the boy asked in astonishment.

"You may think yourself to be clever," said the woodcutter, "but I know you are the thief."

The boy left, but as he did so, he looked back at the woodcutter. The suspicious woodcutter took this as a confirmation of the boy's guilt.

However, the next day, as the woodcutter collected the cut wood, he found his ax lying under the pile of wood. Now when he saw the boy later that day, and looked at his face, it no longer appeared to be that of a thief. It now appeared to be just that of an innocent boy.

This is an old Taoist story, but its message is the same as that of the Yoga Vasishtha, "the world is as you see it." The mind is constantly jumping from one thought to another, one idea to another, like an undisciplined monkey. It is always wavering. But it has a lot of power, and our ideas and concepts color our perception of the world around us. It has the ability to superimpose evil over a good person and even makes one doubt a friend. In fact, it is only the projections of our own undisciplined mind which is the cause of all our difficulties in life.

Earned Food

Once the Buddha went to a farmer for alms, but the farmer got annoyed with him, and rudely said that it was through hard labor that he earned his food.

Buddha quietly told him that he too had earned his bread.

The farmer asked, "If that is so, then where is your plow and oxen?"

The Buddha answered, "The seed I sow is faith, the rain that waters the seed is repentance, wisdom is my plow and yoke, the oxen that draws the plow is diligence; with truth I cut away weeds of sin and ignorance; my harvest is the fruit of immortality."

Gargi and the Sage

The great sage Yajnavalkya had been answering questions in the court of king Janaka for some time when the young Gargi, the daughter of Vacaknu, asked, "O Yajnavalkya, if this whole world is interwoven in the primordial waters lengthwise and crosswise like threads in a cloth, then in what are the waters interwoven lengthwise and crosswise?"

"In the mind, O Gargi," answered Yajnavalkya.

"But then what is the mind interwoven lengthwise and crosswise?" continued Gargi.

"In the world of aerial space, O Gargi." said Yajnavalkya.

"Yes, but in what are worlds of aerial space interwoven lengthwise and crosswise?" Gargi asked.

"In the worlds of the stars," answered Yajnavalkya.

"But in what does the worlds of stars get interwoven," Gargi persisted.

"In the celestial worlds of the gods, O Gargi," said Yajnavalkya.

"Where are the celestial worlds interwoven?" asked Gargi.

"In the worlds of Indra, the king of the gods," answered Yajnavalkya.

"But then where are the worlds of Indra interwoven lengthwise and crosswise?"

"In the worlds of the creator, O Gargi!" said Yajnavalkya.

"But in what is the Creator's world interwoven both lengthwise and crosswise?" questioned Gargi.

"In the worlds of Brahman, the Absolute, O Gargi!" answered Yajnavalkya.

"But then where are the worlds of Brahman interwoven lengthwise and crosswise?" Gargi asked.

"Do not question any further O Gargi," warned Yajnavalkya, "or your head will burst." Yajnavalkya continued, "One can only question up to a point about the Supreme Being. What else can be said of That. It is to be experienced and not discussed, O Gargi."

Hearing the sage's warning, Gargi remained silent. This story teaches us that it is not enough to simply ask questions. We must meditate on their meanings, and should question only after thinking carefully about it. Later, Gargi would pose other questions to the sage, and he answered all of them.

Aja - The Goat

O ne day, all the animals of a local village were out grazing in the forest. But that night, a powerful storm arose, bringing heavy down-pours of rain and wild gusts of wind. Among the animals there was an old goat. He became caught in the storm and wished to find some shelter. He started climbing up a slope until he reached a lion's cave.

The goat went inside, and as the cave was very small, he had to sit with his face looking outside. He was also completely soaked, and his teeth soon started chattering from the cold. He also began to worry, thinking, "This is a lion's den, if he were to return that would surely be my demise."

Meanwhile, while the goat was brooding, the owner of the cave, a young lion cub returned. From a distance, he caught sight of the strange creature sitting in his cave. He had never seen such a creature. He had a long beard like a sage, two horns, and his eyes appeared to glitter.

As the lion cub was still inexperienced, he began to wonder what this creature was. The fact was that the creature was normally food for lions, but the poor lion cub did not know this. And, of course, it is the nature of the mind to take something insignificant and turn it into something more than it is. This is exactly what happened to the young lion. When he saw this creature, he became afraid and kept a respectable distance. The lion cub lost all his courage thinking that no ordinary creature would dare go near his cave, let alone enter it and sit comfortably inside. He therefore called out to the creature asking very humbly, "Sir, who are you?"

The goat was old and very shrewd. Unlike the young lion, he had many years of experience in the game of life. Besides, he knew this might be his last day alive. Therefore, with great firmness he said, "I am the son of *Aja*."

Now in the Sanskrit language, the word *Aja* has two meanings. One meaning is goat, and the other indicates one who is the greatest or most powerful in the world. Already fearful, when the lion cub heard, "The son of Aja," he thought, "Here is the son of the greatest in the world." In a frightened voice the cub said, "What brings you here sir? Please tell me how I can be of service to you."

"I have come to fulfill an important mission," answered the old goat. "That is why I am here," he continued. "You see, my mother did not have any children so she prayed to the great goddess, Mother Kali, promising that if she were blessed with a child, she would sacrifice nine lions to her. Now that I have grown up, I am trying to fulfill that promise on behalf of my mother. I have already sacrificed eight, and now you are going to be the ninth. I will drag you to my home and there sacrifice you as an offering to the goddess."

Upon hearing what the goat had said, the lion cub collapsed in sheer fright. He thought, "This is certainly the end of my life. I will no doubt die very soon."

But then, with folded hands, he prayed to the goat saying, "Kind sir, please listen to my request. I, like you, am the only son of my mother. However, I am still young and have not seen much of the world. I have not even had the opportunity to marry and raise a family yet. Please be compassionate and allow me to live. I would do anything that you ask."

Pretending to be thinking it over, the goat finally said, "Well all right, all right, it doesn't matter. I'll find another lion. I am moved with pity for you. But you must do one thing for me."

"Anything!" answered the lion cub eagerly, "Just name it."

"Well," said the old goat, "you are the king of beasts here and have many subjects. Call an elephant for me so that I may ride him to the village. But there is one condition," continued the goat, "you must not look at me when I ride on top of the elephant. You should also instruct the elephant not to look at me, otherwise the brilliance of my eyes will blind you both."

Being interested only in saving his own life, the lion agreed. He called an elephant and instructed him saying, "Go and stand in front of my cave. There the mighty son of Aja will be waiting. Keep your eyes closed, place him on your back, and take him wherever he wishes to go."

The elephant did as he was told, and as the old goat was climbing on to his back he shouted, "Don't look at me, and make sure your eyes are kept closed." Once he was on his back, the goat directed the elephant towards the village. The lion cub was grateful to be alive and went into his cave.

Meanwhile, the elephant and goat got closer to his village. But just outside the village, some jackals, dogs and wolves were lurking about in search of food. When they saw the goat riding on top of the elephant, they were all amused at the strange sight. And they began shouting at the goat, "It's a good thing you are on the back of that elephant, otherwise we would eat you in an instant."

Hearing their cackles, Aja declared, "One must never stay with the low, but should always be with the great. Although I am a mere goat, by keeping the company of the great lion, I am now riding an elephant. This is indeed the result of keeping the company of the great."

This story illustrates the power and importance of the company one keeps. It is very important to keep the company of those elevated beings who by their mere presence can assist us in achieving our spiritual goals. In life, it is very important to choose the right company, those who can help us fulfill our goals. In the spiritual life, the company of those who have already experienced the inner light of consciousness will also bring us closer to that consciousness as well.

Nasrudin the Siddha

Once Sheikh Nasrudin decided to take a course being given by a wandering *fakir*. It was claimed that the course would teach how to achieve mystical powers (*siddhis*).

The course lasted a whole week, and after it was over, Nasrudin opened his own classroom and put up a sign outside which read: "Sheikh Nasrudin — a man who has acquired a *siddhi*." The Mullah was in fact claiming to have become a *Siddha*, a perfected master with mystical powers.

As word spread of Nasrudin's claim, many of the local people approached him and asked, "Oh Nasrudin, what power have you achieved?"

"I can see in darkness," answered the Mullah.

Well, if this was true, it was indeed a great achievement. Soon many stories of the Mullah's great power spread to even distant towns.

Of course these stories also brought out the skeptics of the area, and they wanted to test Nasrudin's claims. So someone decided to invite Nasrudin for dinner at his home, but said that it would be held at midnight.

Now although it was at an unusual hour, Nasrudin agreed to go. When he started out, it was pitch dark and also drizzling. So he picked up his lantern, lit it, and made his way to the host's house. Along the way, those who had wanted to test him were waiting. So when they saw the Mullah carrying a lantern, they were surprised. They called out to Nasrudin and said, "Oh Nasrudin, you have claimed to be able to see in the dark, but yet you are now carrying a lantern. Why?"

"My dear friends," answered the Mullah with a smile, "Yes, I can see in the dark. But knowing that others cannot, this lantern is meant for your benefit. So you can see me."

Akbar and the Sadhu

Coming to the throne at an early age, Akbar built one of the greatest empires of his time. He lived in magnificent splendor and was surrounded by courtiers who always agreed with everything he said. Because of his great power, the king would sometimes act in an extremely arrogant manner thinking that the whole world belonged to him.

Now Birbal, who was not only the king's minister, but also his friend, decided to teach him something about the nature of this world. That evening, as the king walked through his gardens, he noticed a ragged *sadhu* lying underneath one of the trees. Seeing him, the king became very angry and rushed over to the *sadhu*. He began poking the *sadhu* with the tip of his slipper and shouted, "Wake up! What do you think you are doing? Get out of here at once."

The sadhu opened his eyes and sat up slowly. "Is this your garden?" asked the *sadhu* in a drowsy voice.

"Yes indeed," answered the Emperor, now even more incensed at the *sadhu's* boldness. "This garden, this palace with all its courtyards and forts, this entire empire belongs to me!" said the king.

"The river, along with all of the mountains and cities of India, they all belong to you?" asked the sadhu calmly.

"Yes of course," answered the king, "it is all mine."

"I see," answered the sadhu. "And who owned it before Your Majesty?"

"Why of course my father," answered the king.

Now the king was no longer angry and became interested in the *sadhu's* questions. In fact, the king was a lover of wisdom and enjoyed philosophical discussions of all types. He could tell that the *sadhu* was a learned man and listened to him with greater attention.

"And who was here before your father," the *sadhu* asked further.

"Why his father, my grandfather," answered the king, somewhat impatient, "everyone knows that!"

"Yes of course," replied the *sadhu*. "So this palace, with its forts and gardens, along with all its flowers, bushes and trees, they have all belonged to you for only a short time. Before this, they belonged to your father, and before that to his father. Is that correct?" he asked.

"Yes," agreed Akbar.

"Then it's like a pilgrim's rest house?" the sadhu asked. But he continued without waiting for a response saying, "No one really owns it, but many stay for a short time, and then move on. Or, like a tree along the side of the road, people stop and rest under its shade for awhile and then move on. Many have used it before them and others will come after they have gone. Is this not true?" inquired the *sadhu*.

"It is so," the Emperor agreed.

"So, all these places, your palace and its gardens, in fact your whole empire, will be yours for only the length of your own life. When you are dead, they will no longer belong to you, but will be passed on to your son, just as your father left it to you, and his father to him."

"I see," the king said, now fully appreciating the sadhu's lesson.

"So, what you are saying is that the whole world is like a pilgrim's rest house, and we come and stay for awhile and then move on? And nothing in this world can ever really belong to anyone? This is what you are trying to teach me isn't it?" the king asked.

The *sadhu* nodded his head quietly, and then removed the fake beard and turban he had been wearing. Immediately the king recognized that the *sadhu* was none other than his wise friend Birbal. Akbar was extremely pleased with Birbal's lesson, and he realized that even Emperors are but temporary travelers on the path of life.

I Don't Take My Food
Where I Work

There was once a *sadhu* living alone in a cave. He was tall and robust, and wore only a piece of cloth around his waist. Once, when he was going for his daily collection of alms, a householder, seeing his good physique, asked him why he should not work and earn his food instead of begging for it. The householder told the sadhu that he would be given a meal if he would cut a few logs of firewood which were lying in the householder's yard.

Without saying a word, the sadhu started cutting the firewood with an ax lying nearby, and within a short time he had finished and properly stacked the firewood. Then leaving the ax behind, the sadhu simply walked away.

The householder saw the sadhu leaving and called out to him, asking why he was leaving without taking his meal. "I do not take my food where I work," the sadhu replied, "and I do not work where I take my food."

Sadhus are not allowed to work for their meals. They are supposed to depend on God's grace and the generosity of individuals, and so are not allowed to barter, as one would in a business agreement. The story used to be told by Swami (Papa) Ramdas, the founder of the Anandashram in northern Kerala.

Cat Sannyasa

There was once a cat who was a merciless hunter of rats. All the rats in the community lived in absolute terror of him. But soon he became old, and it became more difficult for him to catch the rats. He therefore had to devise a new strategy.

Now one day, the rats noticed him lying in a motionless position. They watched him for sometime from a distance. But after awhile, when the cat still did not move, the head rat went closer to investigate. Seeing no sign of life, the rat called his brothers and sisters to come closer. They all stood in silence around their old enemy, and wondered if he was dead.

Finally one brave rat reached out and poked the old cat. Slowly the cat opened its eyes, and all the rats drew back in fear. But with a look of shame, the old cat said, "Oh brother rats, I have lived a sinful life. I have been killing and eating your family members for such a long time and have accumulated such bad *karma* that I am thinking of traveling to Benares and ending my life in the sacred Ganges, which they say washes away all of one's sins."

They were astonished at this incredible change of heart in the old cat, so the head rat said, "Oh brother cat, please take us with you to the holy city of Benares, so we too can achieve liberation."

"Aah, dear brother, it will be a long and dangerous journey," the cat warned, "but if you are willing, I will protect you."

The rats readily agreed and they soon started on their long pilgrimage to the holy city, walking in a long line, with the head rat in the front, and the cat bringing up the rear. But as they walked, one by one, the cat killed and ate the last in line, until at last only the chief rat remained. When he looked around and noticed his family members missing, he asked, "Oh brother cat, where are my brothers and sisters?"

But with one look at the cat's face, he suddenly realized what had happened and quickly made his escape.

In India, this is called cat renunciation or sannyasa. Real sadhus warn seekers of such false teachers. One has to be very careful when choosing a Guru, as there are many frauds and deceivers even in the spiritual path.

Nasrudin the Banker

Once Nasrudin decided to become a banker and inaugurated a new bank building. He went about proclaiming that his bank would give loans to any one who asked and without charging any interest. "This bank is here to help the public," announced Nasrudin.

Soon word spread about Nasrudin's promise and a long line formed outside his new bank. Nasrudin was very excited and went out to inspect that everything was going well. When the people saw Nasrudin, they all gathered around him and asked for the various amounts of money they wanted. Nasrudin smiled and said, "Yes, yes, don't worry, you will all get your money."

"But when," asked someone in the crowd.

"As soon as the bank gets some money," Nasrudin answered, "be assured that I will lend it to you."

We must first have money to open a bank. We have to first learn something ourselves before we can teach others. We should try and improve ourselves first before trying to improve others. We have to first imbibe within ourselves the deeper inner state of consciousness before trying to teach others about it.

The Cult of Nose Cutters

Once there was a revengeful thief. After committing a number of robberies, he was finally caught by the authorities. For his punishment, the judge decided to have the man's nose cut off.

But the moment his nose was cut off, the thief began to sing and dance, as if in some sort of ecstasy. Upon seeing this odd behavior, those gathered there asked the man why he appeared so happy after such a gruesome experience.

"Aah," the thief sighed, "it is difficult to convey such a wonderful experience."

"Oh please try," pleaded the crowd.

"Very well," replied the thief, "I will try and communicate it the best I can. You see," the man continued, "the moment my nose was cut off, I immediately had God's vision. Even now I am seeing His glorious form standing before me. And that is why I am dancing with joy."

"But why can we not see Him as well?" asked the people.

"It is because of your noses," answered the thief sadly. "How do you expect to see Him with your noses in the way?" he asked matter of factly.

Now one man in the audience decided to give up his nose in order to have a vision of God. So he asked the thief, "Will you initiate me into your religion?"

The thief pretended to think about it for a moment, and then agreed, "But," he said, "I will do this only in private."

The man agreed and went inside a room with his new master where his nose was instantly cut off. Now it is customary that during initiation, the Guru whispers a sacred *mantra* into the disciple's ear, so the thief also whispered something into the man's ear.

"Unless you want to become a laughing stock," whispered the thief, "do exactly as I have done."

When he realized his stupidity, but not wishing to reveal his embarrassment, the man also began to sing and dance, saying he too saw the Lord standing in front of him.

Soon another person decided to be initiated, then another, and another. Pretty soon there were hundreds who had joined and had their noses cut off. Before long there were at least a thousand of them. They would travel from place to place looking for converts and became known as "the group who show you God."

Now once they stopped in the garden of a local king. When the king heard of their presence, he decided to go and meet them. When the group saw the king approaching, they began to sing and dance as if lost in ecstasy. The king was very impressed and went to meet the group's leader and asked them who they were.

"We are those who show you God," answered the leader.

"Can you show God to me as well," asked the king.

"Yes, but first you must be initiated by having your nose cut off," answered the leader, "otherwise you will not be able to see God. Because it is your nose which blocks your vision of God."

"Very well," answered the foolish king, "I will join your group, along with all my subjects and I will have the court astrologer find an auspicious time for the ceremony."

After saying this, the king returned to his palace. Now the king's Prime Minister was an intelligent man, and he did not agree with the king's decision, but the king would not listen to reason.

When the Prime Minister reached his home, his grandfather, who had himself been the Prime Minister for the king's father, inquired about the day's events at the court. The Prime Minister told his grandfather everything that had happened. When the grandfather heard that the king was about to be initiated into this strange cult, he told his grandson to immediately take him to the palace to see the king.

When they arrived at the palace, the old Prime Minister said, "Your Majesty, don't be in such a hurry to join this group. Think carefully before you do something you may later regret."

But the king's mind had already been made up, and he did not want to hear the old Prime Minister's consul. "With all due respect to your age," the king said, "you don't know what you are talking about. This is a new era, and these people have all seen God. Can a thousand people all be telling a lie?" the king asked.

"Whether they are telling the truth or lying," replied the old minister, "at least investigate it a little further." "After all," he continued, "who in our kingdom has seen God by having their nose cut off?"

"Well, no one that I know of," replied the king.

"Then don't automatically assume that what they claim is true," pleaded the old minister.

The old Prime Minister then made a suggestion saying, "Your Majesty, you are a young man and have many years left to live. I, on the other hand am old and obviously have only a short time left in this world. So let me be the first to have my nose cut off. I will then tell you the truth of whether I see God or not."

The king finally agreed and an auspicious time for the ceremony was set for the next day. The next morning, the old Prime Minister asked the king to have his soldiers posted all around the garden where the group was staying. They then rode out to meet the group's leader.

When they saw the king arriving with all his subjects, the group began to once again sing and dance and got their knives ready. But when the king met with the group's leader, he told him that he should first initiate the old Prime Minister, since he was the eldest of his subjects and should therefore go first out of respect.

The leader of the group agreed, and took the old Prime Minister inside a tent. Then, holding the old man's nose in one hand and the knife in the other, he chopped the nose off with one swift motion. He then whispered into the old man's ear, "Brother, your nose is now gone, and it will never grow back. So, if you don't wish to be laughed at by the whole world, then say that you see God. If you do, everyone will shower respect and wealth on you. If not, you will be a laughing stock."

But the old prime Minister was an honest man, and when he came out of the tent, he walked over to the king and said, "I do not see God but am experiencing only great pain because my nose has been cut off. These people are nothing but rogues. Their leader told me to say that I too saw God, otherwise the world would mock me. Oh king, have your men arrest everyone of them and punish them for their crime."

When the king's soldiers moved in to arrest the group, many began to run and started shouting, "I don't see anything. I don't see anything. I only said that I did because I was told to by our leader." But all where arrested and punished. And so ended the cult of nose cutters.

The Bus Driver and the Preacher

There was once a pompous preacher. Now it so happened that he died at the same time as a simple bus driver. When they reached the gates of heaven, because of his merits, the bus driver was immediately admitted, but unfortunately, the preacher was turned away.

When the outraged preacher asked the gatekeepers why he was turned away and yet the bus driver was admitted, he was informed that his sermons only put people to sleep. But the bus driver drove so recklessly that he inspired all his passengers to pray intensely throughout their entire journey.

Kabir and the Grocer

Although Kabir was himself poor, he was nevertheless an extremely kind and generous man. He had a meager income from the sale of the cloth he weaved but this would allow him to live only from day to day.

One day, during the rainy season, a few holy men unexpectedly showed up at Kabir's door. He naturally welcomed them into his small hut, but because of the rains he had not been able to sell any of his cloth and therefore had no food to offer his guests. He thought that perhaps one of the local grocers could be persuaded to give him some rice and vegetables on credit, so he asked his wife Loi to go to the market and try. But it was doubtful that anyone would give credit to a poor low caste weaver.

Loi went from shop to shop but no one would give her anything on credit. Finally, one grocer agreed to give her the supplies on the condition that she should spend the night with him. Embarrassed at the suggestion, Loi simply smiled, but said nothing. Deluded by his desire, the grocer took this to be a yes, and gave her the groceries.

Loi returned home and prepared a meal for their guests. That evening, after they had left, Loi told Kabir about the grocer's proposal. Kabir thought for a moment and decided to use this opportunity to teach the grocer a lesson about this type of behavior. He told Loi to get ready to go to the grocer. Besides being Kabir's wife, Loi also considered herself to be his disciple, and so she obeyed him knowing his mysterious nature.

Since it was a rainy day, Kabir told her to cover herself with a blanket, and he then lifted her up and carried her to the grocer's shop.

When she went inside, the grocer was surprised to see that her dress and feet were dry and asked her how she was able to get there without getting her feet or dress wet. "My husband covered me with a blanket and carried me on his shoulders to your house," she answered.

Looking at her with disbelief, the grocer began to panic. "Your husband?" he asked nervously.

"Yes," answered Loi, "in fact he is waiting outside to take me home."

Suddenly, the grocer realized the level of depravity that he had sunk to. He fell to his knees and begged Loi for forgiveness. He then asked her to take him to Kabir who also forgave the repentant grocer, and as time passed, he became Kabir's disciple.

Death of the Cauldron

One day Mullah Nasrudin borrowed a large cauldron from one of his neighbors. He used it and returned it the very next day. When the neighbor inspected the pot, he found a small sauce pan inside.

"What is this," the neighbor asked, "there is a small pot inside my cauldron."

"Oh, that," said Nasrudin, "your cauldron has given birth to a little one while in my care. And since you are the owner of the cauldron, by law it rightfully belongs to you."

In thinking that Nasrudin had gone mad, the neighbor remained silent and took both pots.

A few days later, Nasrudin again went to borrow the cauldron. "Why not," thought the neighbor, "perhaps he will leave another sauce pan inside it like the last time." So the neighbor gave Nasrudin the cauldron.

But one day passed, then two, then three days and no sign of Nasrudin and his cauldron. Finally, a week later the neighbor went to Nasrudin's house and knocked on the door. When Nasrudin came to the door he asked, "What do you want?"

"I want my cauldron back," said the neighbor, "you have had

it for a week now."

"I am sorry to tell you," Nasrudin said solemnly, "but your cauldron has died and now lies in its grave."

"What nonsense," the neighbor shouted. "How can a cauldron die?" he asked in disbelief. "Return my cauldron at once!"

"Wait a moment!" said the Mullah. "This is the same cauldron which recently gave birth to a child, a child which is still in your possession, I may add. If a cauldron can give birth, then surely it can die."

Narada's Pride

arada was a great devotee of Vishnu (God). He was also a great practitioner of repeating God's holy name. As he traveled throughout the worlds, Narada repeated God's name twenty-four hours a day. Because of this, Narada became proud of his achievements. He began to think, "People of the world chant God's name for only awhile, but they soon give it up. I, on the other hand, chant it twenty-four hours a day.

Narada soon began to consider himself to be the greatest of God's devotees. So once, while visiting the Lord's heavenly region, Narada asked, "Lord, who is your greatest devotee in all the worlds?"

Of course the Lord came to know of Narada's pride the moment he saw him, so He told Narada to go to a certain place on the earth where there lived a farmer whom He considered as His greatest devotee. The Lord's answer surprised Narada, since he could not understand how the Lord could consider a simple farmer to be His greatest devotee. However, he did as the Lord instructed and went to the farmer's home.

Seeing Narada, the poor farmer was extremely happy and invited the sage to stay with him for sometime. As Narada wanted to observe him, he agreed to the farmer's request. He stayed for a few days watching the farmer's daily routine. He noticed that the farmer got up early each morning and the first thing he did was to loudly call out God's name once. He then went about his daily worldly activities. In the evening, the farmer would do some household chores, and after having his meal, just as he was about to retire for the night, he would once again call aloud God's name.

Now after observing the farmer for a few days, Narada could see nothing remarkable about the man and decided to return to the Lord's heavenly abode. When he reached there, he told the Lord that he could not understand how He could think of the poor farmer as His greatest devotee. "I will show you!" the Lord told Narada.

The Lord picked up a cup and filling it to the brim with milk, told Narada to walk around the celestial palace without spilling a drop of milk. Narada did as he was told and began circumambulating the palace. He walked very slowly, with his mind fully concentrated on the cup of milk. He eventually completed the task without spilling a single drop.

When the Lord saw him, He asked, "Tell me Narada. How many times did you remember me while going around the palace with the cup of milk in your hands?"

"How can you ask such a question?" Narada answered in surprise. My mind was completely concentrated on the cup so I would not spill even a drop of milk. How was it possible to think of anything else?" Narada asked.

Upon hearing Narada's reply, the Lord laughed out loud. "You should consider the case of that poor farmer," the Lord remarked, "he performs many activities throughout the day, and has a number of worldly responsibilities, yet he remembers me at least twice a day without fail. You, on the other hand, completely forgot me while carrying a simple cup of milk."

The Lord's reply went straight to Narada's heart, and he immediately understood the lesson. He realized his mistake in thinking that he was somehow superior to all other devotees. The Lord wanted to show Narada that if someone remembers Him even briefly each day, and then went about performing their daily activities, that person was very dear to the Lord.

Why Ganesh Remained a Bachelor

O ne day, while still a child, Ganesh was playing with his toys when he suddenly saw a cat walking by. In his childish ignorance he grabbed a hold of the cat's tail and began spinning it around as if it were a toy. Although wounded, the poor cat was able to escape with his life.

After he was finished playing, Ganesh went to his mother, who is in fact the Mother of the whole universe. But when he saw her, he noticed bruises on various parts of her body. Surprised at this, he asked her what had happened.

"My child," she answered in a somber mood, "You yourself are the cause of this tragic condition of mine!"

Now Ganesh was extremely devoted to his mother, so when she said this, he began crying and asked, "Oh mother, when did I beat you? I don't recall doing anything which would cause you to suffer in this way."

"Try to remember my son," his mother said searchingly, "and see if you have not beaten any living creature today."

"Why yes," Ganesh suddenly remembered, "Earlier today I beat a cat."

Now Ganesh thought that perhaps the cat's owner had beaten

his mother in retaliation for what he had done to the cat and was now very sorry for his actions. But seeing that he did not understand her, she embraced her son in order to console him and said, "No my son, no one has beaten this body of mine. But since it is I myself who has taken the form of the cat, it is for this reason that you see the marks of your beating on my person. Since you have acted unknowingly, don't worry about it. However, from now on, you should keep in mind that all female forms are parts of me while all males are parts of your father. In fact, there are no persons or things in the whole universe other than Shiva and Shakti."

So from then on, Ganesh always kept this fact in mind. But when he reached marriageable age, he would not agree to get married, since he now saw all women as his mother. He therefore decided to remain celibate all his life. And because of this, he gained great spiritual power and was honored by all the celestials.

Honor Where It's Due

Once Mullah Nasrudin was invited to a wedding reception. But as he was shabbily dressed, everyone ignored him, including the host, the brides father.

Nasrudin quietly slipped out of the side door, untied his donkey and went home. He removed his old clothes and put on his finest robes and returned to the reception. This time everyone greeted him with respect and the host invited him to sit at the head of the table.

"Oh Nasrudin, please sit down," said the host, "and eat and drink."

Nasrudin sat down. When the soup was served, Nasrudin pulled on the sleeve of his robe and began saying, "Eat, coat, eat." Saying this he began dunking the hem of the sleeve into the soup.

Seeing this strange behavior of the Mullah, the host asked, "Oh Nasrudin, what are you doing, what is the meaning of this action?"

"When I arrived wearing my other clothes," explained Nasrudin, "no one offered me anything to eat or drink. But when I returned wearing this fine coat, I was immediately offered the head of the table, as well food and drink. So I can only conclude that it was the coat and not myself who was invited to your banquet. And all the honor you have shown is actually for my robe. So let it eat and have its fill."

Glossary

A

Abhanga: Devotional lyrics or poems written in a particular type of meter in the Marathi language. Saints like Namdev, Nivritti, Jnaneshwar and Tukaram have written literally thousands of *abhangas* which are still sung today.

Aja: From *a* = not + *ja* = born; the unborn Brahman; also the veiling power of God; and the word also means 'goat'.

Ajanabha: According to the Bhagavata Purana, it was the name of India before it became known as *Bharata-varsha*.

Akbar: (1542-1605 C.E.); Great Mogul Emperor who ruled India from 1556 until his death in 1605 C.E. He was a very liberal minded ruler, particularly in areas of religion. His court was open to men of all faiths.

Alauddin: A 13th century Muslim ruler of India who took the throne by having his uncle assassinated.

Amrita: Nectar; the nectar of immortality; the juice tasted by *yogis* when the *kundalini* is awakened and which rejuvenates the body cells.

Apsara: A class of female divinities, sometimes called 'nymphs' who inhabit the heavenly regions. They are said to often visit the earth, and are fond of rivers, lakes, and ponds. They also have the ability of changing their forms at will.

Ashram: Place of striving, from *sram*, 'to exert energy'; a place of refuge from worldly concerns; the abode of a saint or holy man; a spiritual community where spiritual disciplines are practiced; also, a name for the traditional Hindu concept of the four stages of life: 1) student, 2)married life, 3) retirement from worldly concerns, and 4) *sannyasa*.

Ashtavakra: lit. 'bent in eight places'; an ancient sage who was the son of Kahoda and Udalaka muni's daughter. It is said that he was learning the *Vedas* even while in his mother's womb, but he would twist in pain every time his father made a mistake in the recitation, so he was therefore born with eight bends or curvatures in his body. His father, along with a number of other scholars were put to death after being defeated by Bandi, the chief scholar in King Janaka's court. So at the age of twelve, Ashtavakra, who was by then already a renowned scholar went to the king's court and challenged Bandi to a debate, in which he defeated the scholar, and thereby avenged his father's death.

Asura: In early Vedic literature, the word Asura meant a leader of unrivaled qualities, but later it came to refer to demons.

Atman (or Atma): The eternal and unchangeable Self, the inner Spirit; one's true nature or Self. According to the *Brihadaranyaka Upanishad*, the Self should be realized by reflection and meditation after hearing about it from one's Guru.

B

Bharata: The Sanskrit name for India, named after the famous ancient emperor, Bharata; also the loyal brother of lord Rama.

Bheema (or Bhima): One of the five Pandava brothers, and heroes of the great Indian epic the Mahabharata. The five Pandavas were: Yudhishthira, Bheema, Arjuna, Nakula and Sahadeva.

Birbal: A title bestowed by king Akbar, the greatest Moghul emperor, on his close counselor and friend whose original name was Mahesh. The title means, 'one who is wise'.

Brahmin: lit. 'One who knows Brahman'; one of the four main castes according to the ancient Vedic social system. It indicates the spiritual man of society; the man of learning; the teacher and repository of all knowledge.

C

Chintamani: lit. 'the gem of consciousness'; the mythic wish-fulfilling gem used in Indian philosophy to convey the power of the purified mind. It is usually described as being like the green emerald which is ruled by Mercury, the planet representing intelligence.

D

Dervish: A mendicant; a Muslim mystic; a sufi master; a highly evolved spiritual leader in sufi orders; a member of a Muslim order of ascetics, some of which employ circle dancing and chanting in order to produce a collective ecstasy.

Deva: lit. 'shining one'; a celestial being (masculine) and cosmic protector; *div* (Deva) means both 'to shine' as well as 'to play'. According to Brahmanda Purana, the Devas were created by

Brahma while he was in a body which had a predominance of sattva guna. On the other hand, the Asuras were created while Brahma was influenced by a predominance of tamo guna or the quality of darkness and ignorance; the same as Angels in Judaic, Christian, and Muslim religions.

Dinar: Any of several units of gold and silver currency used in the Middle East from the 8th to the 19th century.

G

Ganga (also Ganges): The most sacred river in India today.

Guru, or Guruji: lit. 'one who removes darkness'; a spiritual teacher or preceptor.

Gurudev: lit. 'the divine Guru'; God as Guru; an affectionate, yet respectful term used to address one's Guru.

H

Hanuman: The great monkey devotee of Sri Rama in the Ramayana. He is said to have been the son of the wind god'. He is said to have received his name, which means 'He whose jaw is broken,' when as a child he jumped high into the air trying to catch the Sun. He represents the ideal devotee.

I

Indra: The powerful or mighty; The king, lord, or chief of the gods; Vedic god of rain and thunder; also, in certain Vedic hymns, it means the inner Spirit, the Atman.

J
Jatismara: The name of king Bharata in his next birth as a deer.

Jnaneshwar: lit. 'the Lord of knowledge'; the great 13th century poet/saint of India (1275?-1296), who lived, and is buried in the small town of Alandi near the city of Pune, in modern Maharashtra state. There are two views about his date of birth. One gives the year of birth as 1275 C.E. but Janabai, a close disciple of Namdev, and a contemporary of Jnaneshwar gives the year of birth as 1271 C.E. He is also known as Jnanadeva but the exact Marathi spelling is Dnyanadeo. In the year 1296, Jnaneshwar took *live-samadhi* in front of the Siddheshwara temple in the presence of a large gathering. Shortly after, his younger brother Sopana passed away, followed by his sister Muktabai, and finally Nivrittinatha, his elder brother and Guru. This all occurred within two years of Jnaneshwar's passing.

Julal-ud-Din Rumi (1207-1273 C.E.): Perhaps one of the greatest Sufis and mystical poets in the Persian language. Born in Balkh in Central Asia, at the age of twenty, he obtained a professorship in theology at Konya in Rum (Eastern Anatolia - thus the name Rumi, i.e. 'Byzantine, Roman'). He came under the influence of the famous dervish Shams-ud-Din Tabrizi in 1244, and later, the Sufi, Husam-ud-Din Celebi. Rumi also inspired an independent Sufi order, which became known to European travelers as the 'Whirling Dervishes', which reflects the prominent role of ritual dance in this group's spiritual practices.

K

Ka'ba: The house of *Allah* (God); Islam's most sacred spot; this Arabic word actually means "cube" and indicates the square building housing the sacred stone in the Arabian city of Mecca. All Muslims face Mecca when they pray. The *Ka'ba* was an ancient place of pilgrimage even before Islam. Tradition says that the sacred stone was originally brought to Mecca from Sri Lanka by the Biblical Adam, while others say it was given to Abraham by the archangel Gabriel.

Kabir (1440-1518? C.E.): Great Indian saint who lived in Benares and brought up by Muslim weavers. He came to be known as 'The Weaver saint'. At a young age, he was initiated with the *Ram mantra* from the great saint Ramananda. He taught religious tolerance and would inspire many, even long after his death.

Kalakuta: A deadly poison; the poison of time; a poison said to have arisen during the early stages of the churning of the cosmic ocean by the gods and demons.

Kamadenu: lit. 'the fulfiller of desires'; the name of a wish-fulfilling cow owned by the sage Vasishtha.

Karma: Action or deed, both mental and physical; the law of cause and effect; the reservoir of past impressions; the belief that an individual will reap the fruits of their own past actions, whether in the present life or in some future one; results of one's past actions; destiny; in Vedic times the word was also used to indicate sacred fire rituals (*yajna*).

Kumbha Mela: lit. 'the pot festival'; an ancient spiritual gathering which occurs according to astronomical calculations in a cyclical manner on the banks of sacred rivers at Haridwar, Allahabad, Nashik, and Ujjain.

Kurma: The cosmic tortoise; cosmic stability; a form taken by Lord Vishnu in order to assist in the churning of the cosmic ocean.

L

Lakshmi: The 'beautiful'; One having auspicious marks; the universal mother as the goddess of wealth and prosperity; shakti.

Linga (or lingam): 'Mark, sign, or emblem.' see *Shiva-linga.*

M

Mahatma: lit. "great soul".

Mantra: "instrument of thought"; a mystical or sacred word, verse, or formula given by the Guru at the time of initiation. When given by a Sadguru it is said to be a "conscious" *mantra,* and becomes a vehicle for the transmission of the Guru's spiritual power. *Mantras* may be repeated aloud or silently.

Mullah: An Islamic religious teacher or scholar.

Muslim: lit. "one who surrenders" to God.

N

Namaz: Prostrations; the Muslim prayer which is performed five times a day.

Narada: An ancient sage and devotee of Vishnu (God); The seer of a number of hymns of the Rig Veda and author of several other works, including the Bhakti-Sutras—or aphorisms on Devotion.

Nasrudin: Originally a character used in sufi stories to illustrate the follies of humanity, and Sufi wisdom. Stories of Nasrudin can be found all the way from Greece, the Middle East, and India. Indeed, his tales have traveled the whole world.

Nizamuddin Aulia (1244? – 1325 C.E.): Born in Badaon in northern India, he eventually settled in Delhi, where at the age of twenty-three, he became the head of the Chisti order of Sufis in India, passed on to him by his Guru, Baba Farid. He was a liberal teacher. Amir Khusrau was perhaps his most famous disciple.

P

Prana: lit. 'breathing forth'; vital air; life force or vital energy, from the root *pran*, 'to breathe'; this indicates the life sustaining force of the individual's body, as well as the whole universe. Also, the first of five vital airs (*vayus*). *Prana* in the human body manifests as five vital airs or winds (*vayus*) each performing a specific function, viz., *prana* (outgoing breath) *apana* (incoming breath), *samana* (equalizing breath), *udana* (ascending breath) and *vyana* (separating breath).

Prasad: Purity, grace, blessings; a word which means 'containing blessings or sacred power'; consecrated food, and other offerings, which has been first offered to the deity, saint, or one's Guru; also, anything given by a saint or one's Guru is called *prasad*, such as a gift or a *mantra*.

Prayaga: lit. 'the place of *yajna*'; the ancient name of the North Indian city of Allahabad.

Pushpak: A famed ancient flying machine mentioned in the *Ramayana,* which is said to have flown Rama back to Ayodhya from Sri Lanka after the rescue of Sita.

R

Rama: Hero of the great Indian epic poem, the Ramayana, composed in Sanskrit by the poet Valmiki. Sri Rama is believed to be the 7th incarnation (*Avatar*) of Vishnu (God).

Ravana: A legendary king of Sri Lanka; villain of the Ramayana, who kidnapped Sita, the wife of Sri Rama.

Rishi: 'Seer, sage'; the Vedic seers; a term for an enlightened being emphasizing a visionary wisdom. The Rig Veda mentions seven *rishis* who guide mankind throughout its countless life-cycles.

S

Sadhu: The holy, or virtuous; an ascetic or holy man. From *sadh*, meaning 'one who goes straight to the goal.' According to Add Shankaracharya, a *sadhu* is one who is endowed with *sattva-guna*, the quality of purity, who has good conduct, and who is well versed in every branch of learning. A *sadhu* may or may not be a yogi or *sannyasin*.

Sanjivan: The art of restoring life or bringing one back from the dead.

Sannyasin: lit. one who "throws down or abandons"; one who has renounced or abandoned the worldly life in favor of the monastic life. *Sannyasa* is a personal dedication to the path of God-Realization and service to humanity.

Shesha: lit. 'the remainder'; the residue or remainder of the universe during cosmic dissolution; the king of serpents; the cosmic serpent; also known as Ananta.

Shiva: lit. 'the auspicious, kind, gracious or compassionate One'; the name given to the Absolute when viewed as the dissolver of the universe; according to Shaivism, the Supreme Lord who is transcendent, as well as immanent. In His immanent form, He is the Creator, Preserver and Destroyer of the universe.

Shiva-linga: An emblem, mark or sign of Shiva; a symbol representing the Absolute Being in his unmanifested state. A rounded, elliptical, aniconic image made of stone, metal, crystal, wood, or any natural substance, either carved or natural.

Sita: Wife of Lord Rama. Sita was kidnapped by Ravana, and Rama had to rescue her. The story is retold in the epic *Ramayana*.

So'Ham: lit. 'That I Am'; the natural mantra which is going on within each individual. Also, Ham'Sa.

Sufis: The mystics within the religion of Islam. From *suf*, 'wool', indicating the simple woolen robe worn by the Sufis.

Sukracharya: The preceptor of the demons; the planet Venus; he is said to have had the knowledge of the art of reviving the dead, known as *Sanjivani.*

T

Tamasa: One of the three qualities (*gunas*) of primordial Nature (*Prakriti*), which are Sattva, Rajo, and Tamo guna; the quality of ignorance, delusion, and inertia.

Taxila: A famous crossroads of the ancient silk road located in modern Pakistan. It was also a well known center of learning some two thousand years ago.

U

Upanishad: lit. 'sitting near'; also meaning, 'esoteric knowledge'; the scriptures embodying the teachings of the ancient sages of India and which are a part of the Vedas. Traditionally, the number of Upanishads is given as 108, but only ten to sixteen are considered to be 'major' or 'principle' Upanishads.

V

Valmiki: lit. 'born of an anthill'; a great sage and poet; the author of the Indian epic, the *Ramayana.* After leading the life of a highwayman robbing and even killing his victims, he was given the mantra '*Rama*' by the seven rishis who he tried to rob. He began to repeat the mantra with such intensity that he remained seated in one position for such a long time that his body became covered by an anthill created by white ants. Besides writing the world famous Ramayana, he is also credited with writing the Yoga Vasishtha, which is the Vedantic teachings of Sage Vasishtha to Sri Rama.

Varsha: Land, country.

Vedanta: lit. 'ultimate knowledge, the final conclusion of the Vedas'; Vedic philosophy or knowledge indicating ultimate wisdom; one of the six orthodox schools of Indian philosophy arising from discussions in the Upanishads about the nature of the Absolute. The three main scriptures of this philosophy are: the Upanishads, Brahma Sutras, and the Bhagavad Gita.

Vishnu: All pervasive; omnipresent; A name given to the Absolute when viewed as the sustainer of the universe; He is conceived of as having his special abode in the realm, or heavenly region known as Vaikuntha.

Vithoba (same as Vitthal): A corrupt form of Vishnu; the name of the deity in the famous temple of Pandharpur in the modern state of Maharashtra, India.

Y

Yajnavalkya: An ancient sage of the Vedic period. His teachings are found in the Brihadaranyaka Upanishad.

Yaksha: A supernatural being; a demigod; a class of semi-divine beings who are the attendants of Kubera, the treasurer of the gods.

Yama: the 'Restrainer'; The name of the god of death. He is also known as the god of justice (Dharma).

Yoga: lit. 'union'; from *yuj*, to 'yoke or join'; one of the six systems of Hindu philosophy. Yoga teaches the means by which the individual spirit can be joined or united with the Universal Spirit.

Yogadanda: A 'T' shaped stick, approximately 18 inches high used by yogis to lean on during long periods of japa and meditation.

Yogi: A male practitioner of yoga; also, one who has achieved yoga or union; a Yogini is the female equivalent.

Z
Zipruanna: A great Siddha and friend of Swami Muktananda belonging to Nashirabad, in the state of Maharashtra, India.

Mail-in-Order-Form

Sarasvati Production

1625 Hollingsworth Dr.
Mountain View, CA 94040-2950 (USA)
(650) 386-6265
www.SarasvatiProductions.com

Ask the Horse!
And More Stories My Guru Told Me

ISBN: 978-1-886140-14-1
6x9 - 272 pages - $18.95

Ask the Horse!
– And More Stories My Guru Told Me
Retold by Swami Prakashananda

Please make check or money-order payable to: Sarasvati Productions

Ship Order To:

— **Please Print Clearly** —

Name_____

Address_____

City _____ State_____ Zip Code_____

Telephone _____ e-mail_____

Title	Quantity	Price per copy	Total
Ask the Horse!		$18.95	
California residents add 8.25% Sales Tax ($1.56 for each book)			
USPS Media Mail (1-2 weeks*) - $3.95 for 1st book & $1 for each additional book			
USPS Priority Mail (3-4 days) - $7.95 for 1st book & $1.50 for each additional book			
		Grand Total	

* Please allow up to 2 to 3 weeks for delivery in the Continental US and as long as 6 weeks to Hawaii.